THE COMPLETE
## CABIN CREW
INTERVIEW
MANUAL

THE COMPLETE
# CABIN CREW
## INTERVIEW
### MANUAL

The Complete Cabin Crew Interview Manual

First Edition by Elizabeth James
Copyright © 2018 Elizabeth James
All rights reserved.

Published by:
The Airline Career Insitute
United Kingdom

ISBN: 978-1-908300-30-0

Printed in the United Kingdom
10 9 8 7 6 5 4 3 2 1

Library of Congress Cataloging-in-Publication Data
A CIP catalogue record for this book can be obtained from the British Library

### Cover Photography Credits

| | |
|---|---|
| Photographer: | Andrey Yakovlev |
| Art Director: | Tat'yana Safronova |
| Model: | Marina Azarova |
| Style, Makeup: | Lili Aleeva |
| Hair Style: | Ovo Arakelyan |

© CC- BY-ND 2012 Andrey Yakovlev & Lili Aleeva

With special thanks to AeroFlot Airlines

> "Who said it could not be done? And what great victories has he to his credit which qualify him to judge others accurately?
> - *Napoleon Hill*"

# PART 1

## THE INSIDE SCOOP

**1**   The truth about the hiring process    Page 21

**2**   Uncovering the true assessment criteria    Page 33

Unveiling the hidden criterion - Age - Marital status and family life
Personal appearance - Gender - Personal bias - Avoid being culled

**3**   Secret screenings and booby traps    Page 43

Your fate and the red pen - The awkward silence - Secret spies
Colour-coded sticky notes - The friendly interviewer routine
The lull of reciprocation - The guise of a positive question
The abrupt end - The telephone screening trap

**4**   Undercover operations    Page 55

Hidden assessments - It's not what you think - Shocking revelations
Innocent casualties and bystanders - What to expect
Your greatest ally - Create the right impression - The lineup
The unusual suspects - Handling questions and dialogue

# PART 2

# MAKE YOURSELF UNFORGETTABLE

### 5   Polish your appearance   Page 81

Debunking the myths - The all-important first impression
Misconceptions & misinterpretations - Stand out by not fitting in
Style guide: Ladies - Style guide: Gents - Appearance concerns

### 6   Create the right impression   Page 105

Consider your communication - Let your body do the talking
The eyes definitely have it - Caution: Smokers

### 7   Create a memorable impression   Page 119

The art of the connection - Mirror, mirror - Leading - Disconnection
How to pull it off - The one type who always gets the offer
Just like old friends - The enthusiastic approach

# PART 3

## SURVIVAL 101

### 8  Resolve common concerns — Page 137

Blushing - Cottonmouth - Excessive sweating - Eye contact
Going blank - Involuntary facial motions - Vocal paralysis
Fidgeting - Perceived arrogance - Being alienated - Being ridiculed
Handling disagreements - Feeling uncertain

### 9  Manage your nerves — Page 151

Manage your mindset - Use your imagination - Anchor your state
Ask resourceful questions - Adjust your physiology - Find your focus
Create compelling reasons - Affirm and incant

### 10  Bloopers, blunders & faux pas recovery — Page 167

It happens to the best of us - Three effective approaches
The smooth recovery - The artful apology
Be willing to laugh at your own expense
It's how you handle it that counts

# PART 4

## BOOST YOUR CANDIDACY

### 11 Application guidance — Page 177

Ulterior motives - Important guidelines - Stretching the truth
Minimise a fragmented work history - Fill gaps in employment
Never admit to being fired - Age discrimination
Communicate your suitability - Use action phrases
Leverage your leisure interests - The power of a personal statement
Highlight career progression - List your awards
Get permission from your referees - Application example

### 12 Resume guidance — Page 197

Influence the direction of the interview - Appearance
A computer could be deciding your fate - Action verbs - Format
Outline - Sample resume

### 13 Produce polished photographs — Page 213

Requirements - Formal vs Informal - Set the Scene - Work the Angles
Dress the Part - Tend to your Grooming - Warm your Smile

### 14 Power up your portfolio — Page 221

Boost your experience - Get volunteer work - Learn new skills -
Enhance your education - Engage in extra-curricular activities

# PART 5

# LIFTING THE LID ON THE GROUP INTERVIEW

 What to expect — Page 231

Complacency and the waiting game - Just a number
Avoid the traps during the icebreaker session
Stand out as an individual - A process of elimination

 Hidden meanings behind the group tasks — Page 245

What recruiters are really looking for - Where confusion often occurs
Focusing on the wrong element - Seven heavenly virtues
Seven deadly sins - Active involvement is essential...
...But don't overdo it - Your scorecard

 Sample tasks — Page 261

Practical Tasks - Group Discussions - Role Play Scenarios

# PART 6

# TAKE ON THE FINAL INTERVIEW

### 18  What to expect — Page 279

Icebreaker or deal-breaker - Meet the recruitment team
What assessors are really looking for - Seven Heavenly Virtues
Seven Deadly Sins - Avoid robotic, flat and boring answers
Demonstrate respect for the recruiters - Eek, I don't know the answer
Run of the mill cliche's will not cut it - Stand out as an informed candidate

### 19  Winning formula — Page 295

Answers as easy as A.B.C - A.C.T on negative questions
Winning answers with S.A.R.R formula
Probing with follow-up questions - The constant interruption

### 20  Guidelines for the most frequent questions — Page 307

### 21  Sample answers — Page 355

Behavioural - Traditional

### 22  Ask the right questions — Page 389

Question Guidelines - Questions about Suitability
Questions about the Recruiter - General Questions - No Questions
Questions to Avoid

# Disclaimer
## FROM THE PUBLISHER

This book is designed to provide information and guidance on attending a cabin crew assessment. It is sold with the understanding that the publisher and author are not engaged in rendering legal or other professional services. Such topics, as discussed herein are, for example, or illustrative purposes only. If expert assistance is required, the services of a competent professional should be sought where you can explore the unique aspects of your situation and can receive specific advice tailored to your circumstances.

It is not the purpose of this guide to reprint all the information that is otherwise available to candidates but instead to complement, amplify and supplement other texts. You are urged to read all the available material, learn as much as possible about the role and interview techniques and tailor the information to your individual needs.

Every effort has been made to make this guide as complete and accurate as possible. However, this guide contains information that is current only up to the printing date. Interview processes are frequently updated and are often subject to differing interpretations. Therefore, there are no absolutes and this text should be used only as a general guide and not as the ultimate source of information.

All information in this book is offered as an opinion of the author and should be taken as such and used with discretion by the reader. You are solely responsible for your use of this book. Neither the publisher nor the author explicitly or implicitly promises that readers will find employment because of anything written or implied here.

The purpose of this guide is to educate and inform. The author and The Airline Career Institute shall have neither liability nor responsibility to you or anyone else because of any information contained in or left out of this book.

**The views and opinions expressed within this guide are those of the author and do not represent the views of any airlines or organisations named within. Any airlines mentioned are for the purpose of demonstration only. This book is neither associated, approved, affiliated with, nor endorsed by any airline.**

# My Dedication

## TO YOU

This book is dedicated to all my readers who refuse to give up on their dream.

Thank you and good luck

# THE
# INSIDE SCOOP
## PART 1

# Contents
## Of this Session

1. The truth about the hiring process

2. Uncovering the true assessment criteria

3. Secret screenings & booby traps

4. Undercover operations

> "You can do it, if you believe you can"
>
> *- Napoleon Hill*

# THE
# TRUTH
## ABOUT THE HIRING PROCESS

# The truth ABOUT THE ~~HIRING~~ elimination PROCESS

We'd all like to think that recruitment personnel are giving their undivided attention to each resume they receive, and we'd also like to think that every candidate would receive a fair and equal opportunity to interview for the position. The unfortunate truth is, each airline receives thousands of applications every month. This not only puts a great deal of pressure on recruitment teams to reduce the load, but also makes it very difficult for any one candidate to stand out.

After seeing hundreds of hopefuls, it is only natural that faces and resumes begin to blur, with each sounding and looking much the same as the next.

*"The process is designed to filter and eliminate"*

To address this overload, airlines have become highly selective and candidates are put through a gruelling screening process, whereby **hidden assessments** and **trick questions** provide recruitment personnel an opportunity to **secretly eliminate** large numbers of unsuspecting candidates as early as possible. In essence, the process is no longer one that is designed to screen for the right candidate or the best fit, but rather to filter and eliminate.

What was once a merely challenging process has morphed into a barrage of **trick questions, underhand tactics, psychological traps, and secret criteria.** Each designed to whittle down the numbers as quickly as possible, leaving those candidates who are unprepared and uninformed feeling bewildered and confused by the whole process.

# It's not fair

While this process sounds unfair and brutal, it is not intended to be cruel or malicious. Rather, it has become an unavoidable means of conducting high volume and fast paced interviews within the majority of airlines. In order to understand the motives behind such recruitment processes, it helps to understand things from the airline and recruitment officer's perspective. So, let's consider the following statistics:

In 2012, Delta Air Lines received **22,000 applications for just 300 openings,** with applications arriving at a rate of 2 per minute. (Bloomberg: 2012) This is not an abnormal occurrence as Delta has also been quoted to receive **100,000 for 1,000 jobs** just 2 years earlier (ABC News, 2010). These statistics put each applicant at less than **2% chance of success.**

Meanwhile, Emirates Airline is "Swamped with cabin crew applications" (Gulf News, 2010).

*"Applications arriving at a rate of 2 per minute"*

Today Emirates are quoted to recieve over **15,000 applications each and every month,** with most recruitment drives attracting over 1,000 candidates. It is also recorded that, of the 400 candidates who turned up to a 2010 open day in Spain, **just 30 made it though** to the final interview. The Chief Commercial Officer of Emirates, Thierry Antinori, noted that **Emirates received over 129,000 applications** during 2013. (Trade Arabia, 2014)

Similarly, Al Baker of Qatar Airways reports "Qatar Airways was recruiting 250-300 cabin crew every month and that each open recruitment session saw around **800-2,500 candidates.** (Reuters, 2014)

As you can now appreciate, conducting recruitment drives on such a large scale is a tedious task for the personnel who oversee the process, not to mention an expensive one for the airline.

# Hidden strategies
## AND DECEPTIVE TACTICS

**So, why donít airlines just recruit additional staff to handle the load?**

All companies, not just airlines, are aware that candidates rarely show their true selves during a formal interview process. After all, it is only natural that candidates want to be seen in the best possible light. The problem is that some candidates will go so far as to put on a show in order to impress, and even mislead, the officers. These make it difficult for recruitment personnel to accurately gage whether a candidate truly is a good fit for the airline and its corporate culture, or is just playing the part for the interview.

Sadly, more recruitment personnel do not address this problem, so airlines have come up with an alternative strategy: A strategy that not only restores the power of control back to the airline, but also relieves the uncertainty.

*"Airlines have come up with an alternative strategy"*

# Hidden surveillance
## AND UNDERCOVER OPS

The fact is, additional recruiters have already been hired, however, these additional members of the team are not part of the identifiable personnel, but are part of the **undercover team**.

To help the recruitment officers make informed decisions and better elimination choices, undercover officers are often placed among the group during recruitment days. Within the guise of a fellow candidate, these officers can observe individuals in their relaxed and natural state, and be in a better position to extract information.

Information that would never otherwise be revealed is openly volunteered by unsuspecting candidates, as they are **lulled into a false sense of security and tricked into dialogue with deadly small talk**. Any mishap can land your resume in the rejection pile and you to the nearest exit.

These officers are largely accountable for the high percentage of failure rates that candidates experience during the group stage and are the reason why many candidates leave the interview feeling confused about their elimination. More significantly, it is those **friendly manipulation and underhand tactics** that enable officers to uncover information and eliminate candidates based on **secret criteria and other discriminations**.

*"Information that would never otherwise be revealed is openly volunteered by unsuspecting candidates"*

# Secret criterion
## AND DISCRIMINATIONS

It is no secret that airlines have stringent criteria for their cabin crew recruits. Among these, you will find minimum and maximum age, height and weight ranges, as well as health, fitness and grooming guidelines. These criteria are openly published and accessible to candidates through the airlines literature, however, **what candidates don't know, and what airlines will never reveal, are the secret criteria for which many elimination decisions are based.**

This secret criterion goes far beyond what is essential for the safe and effective conduct of the cabin crew duties, and even beyond what is considered ethical and moral. With no legal requirement to tell candidates why they were unsuccessful, most airlines have adopted a **zero feedback policy**. While this policy has been put in place due to the sheer volume of applicants, the protection this policy provides, sadly, leaves it **open to abuse.**

Every airline, from the largest international carriers to the smallest national operators, has its own **secret screening criteria**. As such, it is important to remember that, although it is illegal to discriminate, anything you share with the airline or their staff can be used against you without your knowledge. In such instances, these decisions can never be challenged or verified because such criterion are never openly discussed, nor are they written dawn. Essentially, they don't officially exist.

*"Every airline has its own secret screening criteria"*

# Inconsistent
## AND CONFUSING OUTCOMES

This lack of coherence and transparency naturally leads to very inconsistent outcomes for unsuspecting candidates, who may be viewed favourably by one officer, but not the next. Such exclusions appear to be without just cause, **leaving candidates confused and dejected** by the whole process.

*"Unaware of the hidden processes that lie deep within the screeening process"*

As the candidate struggles to establish a logical explanation for their dismissal, they tend to fall into a deadly cycle of overanalysing their own performance, often becoming overly self critical and then coming to the wrong conclusion entirely: A conclusion, which is often **taken out of context and to the extreme**. This leads to yet another problem, the problem of self-doubt and lack of confidence.

In the quest for answers, such candidates often seek out the comfort and guidance of others. Unfortunately, however, the guidance they receive is often from others who are just as confused as they are, as they too are unaware of the hidden processes that lie deep within the screening process. Sadly, this is also where the **myths and fear mongering** emerge, leaving the candidate feeling helpless and ready to give up on their dream.

# The flaws
## IN THE SYSTEM

For the most part, the motives behind employing these strategies are understandable. With the high costs incurred from the recruitment drives, not to mention the expense associated with the training and licensing of new hires, It goes without saying that **any mistakes made in the hiring process work out to be a very expensive and time consuming ordeal for the airline:** An ordeal that airlines will do anything to avoid.

*"Under pressure to whittle down the numbers"*

The unfortunate thing is that **it is often the innocent candidates who lose out** with such a system. This is because undercover officers are under such a great deal of pressure to whittle down the numbers, that **elimination decisions can be based on minor and negligible reasons.**

For instance, most candidates will experience some form of anxiety during an interview. While such a phenomenon is entirely natural and forgivable during the early stages of the process, the outward symptoms may cause a temporary shift in the candidate's personality. While this is not a accurate representation of their true character, the candidate may be eliminated before they have chance to compose themselves.

Unfortunately, this is a process that is unlikely to change as long as demand for cabin crew positions continue to increase. So rather than be discouraged by this flawed system, **it is time to take control** so that you can **work this system to your advantage.**

# Work the system
## TO YOUR ADVANTAGE

By understanding the process from the inside, **you can avoid being slaughtered by these underhand tactics.** You can tip the balance of power in your favour, so that you become the one who is doing the screening, not the airline. **No longer will you be cursed with generic run-of-the-mill answers and uninspiring resumes that have you looking and sounding like everyone else,** but will stand out as the top candidate that you truly are.

So whether you are a seasoned applicant who is finding yourself frustrated by another unsuccessful attempt or are a new candidate looking forward to your first interview, the **insider secrets and step by step guidance** within this book will give you a huge lead over the competition.

*"No longer will you be cursed with generic answers and uninspiring resumes"*

# Discover
## THE HIDDEN SECRETS

You will not find pages of information informing you about the duties, history and roster structures, and nor will you find average advice. **This book is raw and will take you behind the scenes to reveal secrets that airlines donít want you to know.**

The information is **universal**, revealing how candidates are screened and hired all across the world, from the largest international carriers to the smallest national operators. The information is **timeless**, so you will not find outdated or irrelevant advice, and, most importantly, it is **uncensored**. For the first time, you be shown how to avoid the common traps and pitfalls, and the true reasons why no airline will ever tell you why you were unsuccessful in your pursuit.

The hiring process is not always correct and it is often unfair, however, if you **understand the process from the inside**, you will never have to worry about what is expected or what recruiters really want to hear, You can enter the process informed and prepared, ready to come away with the job offer.

*"Prepare yourself, for you are about to understand the screening process from an entirely different perspective."*

" Don't worry about failures. Worry about the opportunities you miss when you don't even try "

*- Jack Canfield*

# THE TRUE
## ASSESSMENT CRITERIA

## ASSESSMENT CRITERIA

If you visit any airline website, you will find the criteria for the position of cabin crew is openly published and available to view. The guidelines are very simple and often outline key elements, which fall into the following categories Eligibility, suitability and specific criteria.

Most candidates will find these guidelines very easy to qualify for, and most will exceed those given. So, why is the success rate for cabin crew so very low? The answer lies within the fourth criterion.

# Unveilling the hidden criterion

This fourth criterion is the hidden element that airlines don't publish and don't want candidates to know. This is because the hidden criterion actually falls within the realms of discrimination. While such prejudices are considered illegal in most countries, it is unfortunate that these still do occur within most industries and organisations worldwide.

This discriminatory practice is able to continue because of the layer of protection afforded by the airlines 'no feedback' policy. Candidates can be eliminated for any reason at all, even if that reason is immoral, unethical or illegal, simply because they are never openly discussed and nor are they written dawn.

While some of these criterion are indicative of issues that cannot be overcome or changed, many of these are absolutely within your control and there are strategies that you can use to protect yourself from being culled under these circumstances.

So let's take a look at what you may be up against.

# Age barriers

Due to regulations, many airlines no longer advise an upper age limit as part of their criteria; however, this does not mean that none exist. In fact, it is quite the contrary. Until recently, many airlines did advise an upper age limit, typically in the mid to late 50s, however this was rarely their preference and did not imply such candidates would be given a fair and equal opportunity.

Nowadays, airlines often imply 'young', 'youthful' and 'energetic' as part of their job description, in order to attract younger applicants, and officers are able to eliminate mature candidates at will.

Unfortunately, age discrimination does not end there. If you are a female of childbearing age, you may also face discrimination, even if you have no intention or desire to have a child. This is evidenced by the 2013 campaign by GoAir, the low cost Indian airline, which openly advertised for candidate's between18-24 years old (WSJ, 2013).

While this level of honestly is rare, it does provide a valuable insight into what really goes on behind the scenes.

# Marital Status
## AND FAMILY LIFE

Female candidates face further scrutiny when it comes to their family life, marital status and childbearing plans. It is assumed that female crew who have family commitments are inflexible and have priorities, which run contrary to those of the position. Worse still are the assumptions made that female crew in their 30s will be likely to leave quickly due to marriage and childbearing plans.

Qatar airlines are so strict when it comes to personal relations, that they even go as far as to prohibit marriage within the first five years of employment. (Reuters, 2014)

**Beware**: Wearing a wedding band or engagement ring is a clear indication of your marital status, as is a picture of your child being revealed as you access your belongings.

# Personal
## APPEARANCE

While it is a myth that airlines only hire candidates who embody perfect figures and harbour model looks, there is no denying that airlines do favour candidates who are well groomed and portray a polished image. Candidates who arrive un-groomed or in less than desirable attire are unlikely to continue far in the process, as are those who are sporting visible tattoos or facial piercings, outrageous hair colours or styles.

For those of you who are blessed with above average appearance, it will certainly not harm your candidacy; however, do not be disillusioned that this aspect alone will provide you with an automatic admission. Such ideas will only lead you into a false sense of security and disappointment.

Another aspect of appearance that often comes up is with reference to weight. For this purpose, airlines refer to the Body Mass Index (BMI) guidelines.

The BMI is a formula used by health professionals to determine an adult's healthy body weight in relation to their height. While weight is an avenue that is certainly open to discrimination, particularly for those who fall within the higher end of the spectrum, it is unlikely to be a problem if your weight falls within the mid to lower parameters of the chart. You can determine your own proportions, by referring to the BMI chart that follows.

## Body Mass Index (BMI) Chart for Adults

| Region | BMI |
|---|---|
| Obese | BMI 30 & Above |
| Overweight | BMI 25-30 |
| Normal | BMI 18.5-25 |
| Underweight | BMI < 18.5 |

Height (no shoes)

© 2009 Vertex42 LLC

- BMI Chart created by Vertex42.com. Used with permission.

| BMI | Category |
|---|---|
| <20 | Underweight |
| 20 – 25 | Normal weight |
| 26 – 29 | Slightly Overweight |
| >30 | Overweight |
| | Extremely Overweight |

39

# Gender

Another discrimination that has been highlighted recently is that of gender. The reason for this discrimination is down to the costs associated with weight management. The rationale is that men are often heavier than their female counterparts. This was first brought to light when GoAir disclosed "significant savings of over £330,000 from hiring female only crew" (Daily Mail, 2013).

Whether this is something that we can see spreading to other airlines is uncertain, however, it is important to be aware of such exclusions if you are a male candidate.

# Personal Bias

This criteria is much more difficult to define, simply because these are generally open to the interpretation and discretion of the recruitment personnel. Under this criterion, a candidate may be subjected to outright discrimination, the victim of a personality clash or for no logical reason at all.

Such biases are not defined by the airline, and often times the airline isn't even aware of their existence. They are the views harboured on a personal and individual level and not necessarily the consensus on any of the other recruitment personnel.

Unfortunately, such decisions can never be challenged or verified because they don't officially exist.

# Avoid being culled

It may or may not surprise you to discover that the risk of being eliminated based on such discriminations is often within your power. Often times, a candidate is eliminated simply because of his or her own willingness to share such personal and private information. Candidates don't realise that secret eliminations and discriminations occur and nor are they aware that undercover officers are patrolling the floor extracting information from unsuspecting candidates. It is this sharing of information that inadvertently causes many candidates to be secretly and unfairly screened out from the process.

Let us take age as an example. The information represented on your resume is an easy way for recruiters to decipher your age. So, in order to conceal this, you may consider omitting dates and providing only a partial employment history. Problem solved, right? Not quite. Personnel are trained to use a variety of tactics to get you to volunteer sensitive information that would be illegal to ask in an interview. In the absence of solid information, it is the undercover recruitment personnel, trick questions and friendly manipulation that come into play.

Due to the legality of such discriminations, it is highly unlikely that you will be asked any of these questions outright. What is most likely is that the questions will come in the form of icebreakers or a friendly small talk. As such, it is important to remember that, although it is illegal to discriminate, anything you share with the airline or their staff can be used against you without your knowledge and without any evidence to dispute. So always be on guard with your sensitive information and always keep your personal life personal.

As we progress onto the upcoming sections of this book, I will go into much more detail about these undercover operations and how you can avoid falling victim to their manipulation. So continue reading...

" A successful man is one who can lay a firm foundation with bricks others have thrown at him "

*- David Brinkley*

# SECRET SCREENINGS
## AND BOOBY TRAPS

# Your fate
## AND THE red pen

Turning up to a cabin crew interview without a pen could spell disaster for your pursuit. Not only will you look unprepared, but the apparent lack of intention to take down any notes will give the impression that you are not serious.

For this reason, the recruiters will carry a supply of red, or green, pens so that they can easily identify such candidates when it comes time for processing the eliminations. Needless to say that any forms completed in red or green ink will be immediately rejected.

To avoid this very simple blunder, it is always best to carry two pens. This will provide you with a backup should one run out of ink or become lost, or you may need to help out a fellow candidate in their time of need. Just be sure that both pens contain either blue or black ink.

# The Awkward
## SILENCE

One of the most common interview traps you will encounter is the silent treatment. With this trick, the interviewer will respond to your answer with a blank stare and a deadening silence. This trick is so incredibly effective because most candidates are so intimidated by silence that they will often rush to fill the void.

Rather than see the silence as just a pause for thought, many candidates will view the silence as an indication that they have just goofed up in some way. It is in their haste to justify and recover their answer that they then volunteer irrelevant or damaging information, often appearing flustered and knocking themselves out of contention.

The point of using silence is to see how you respond to stress, therefore, whenever you are confronted with silence, the best strategy is to remain silent yourself. If the silence persists after 5-10 seconds, you can proceed to ask "is there anything I can add to clarify this point?" or "Did I answer the question fully enough?" These questions will demonstrate that you are not intimidated by silence or stress and will put the responsibility clearly back onto the interviewer. If there is something troubling him or her, this will encourage disclosure and an appropriate opportunity for you to reiterate.

# Secret spies

Whenever you are in the vicinity of the airline's territory, you will want to be watchful of your surroundings. Whether you are in the waiting area, at the front desk or in the restroom it is a good bet that employees, who have been enlisted to become internal spies for the recruitment team, are observing you.

The most obvious, yet often overlooked, internal spy is that of the humble receptionist. As the first and last point of contact, these powerful gatekeepers are in a prime position to observe candidates in all circumstances and from every angle. In putting on the friendly receptionist routine they are able to engage candidates in friendly dialogue, gathering information that can then be fed back to the recruitment team. Taking on a different approach, such as being rude or ignoring your presence, they will be able to entice and observe a different reaction entirely: A reaction that would otherwise not be accessible.

And what about the seemingly harmless cleaning staff in the restroom? Could they also be used for such purposes? Absolutely. In fact, It is within the so-called privacy of the restroom that candidates often vent their frustrations or bare their souls. So it is important to always be mindful of your interaction with anyone you come into contact with, even your fellow candidates. As we venture into the section entitled 'Undercover Ops', we will explore this aspect much further.

# Colour-coded sticky notes

When it comes to feeding information back to the recruitment team, the receptionists use secret signals in the form of colour-coded sticky notes. If any red flags or doubts are raised about any candidate, a specific colour sticky note will be placed on their application form as a forewarning. If this happens, the candidate may be awarded a courtesy interview, but this is often as far as they will go.

Due to the nature of this trick, it is often reserved for the invitation only or final interview sessions.

# The friendly
## INTERVIEWER ROUTINE

The friendly interviewer routine is one that catches even the most seasoned candidates off guard. You enter the interview room and are surprised to discover that you are greeted by a warm and friendly welcome. The interviewer chats openly about all sorts of things, almost as if you are just catching up with an old friend. They make you feel at ease and, as you feel like you are starting to make a connection with this friendly individual, you suddenly find yourself letting your guard down.

Maybe you feel that you've created some sort of friendship. Maybe this interviewer is looking to help you get a job. Wrong! Interviewers are trained to be enthusiastic and friendly representatives of the airline, and it is this friendly approach that lulls candidates into a false sense of security. Under these relaxed conditions the interviewer is able to get a better sense of who you really are, and before you know it you begin revealing sensitive information about your home life, financial problems, health, former employer and challenges you are facing. By the time you realise that you've said too much, it's already too late.

Whenever you meet the interviewer for the first time, it is important not to be taken in by this friendly approach. You certainly don't to want to appear rigid, by any means, but you do need to be mindful of who you are talking to and remain professional.

# The lull of reciprocation

Following on from the friendly interviewer routine is the lull of reciprocation tactic. This tactic is probably one of the sneakiest because it is very easy to be taken in if you are unprepared. Here's how it works:

You enter the interviewer's office and the officer casually begins to open dialogue with some small talk about their children, or complains about their knee as they struggle to take their seat. Harmless? Unfortunately not! The purpose of this dialogue is to encourage a reciprocal response. For those candidates who are parents themselves, it is only natural that they too will begin to talk about your own children in response to such a comment. Or if a candidate is facing health struggles of their own, they may feel compelled to share out of empathy or politeness. 3178

These are just two examples, but there could be many more related to age, marital status, or your employment history. The list could go on.

Reciprocal remarks are quite acceptable in a social setting, but are completely inappropriate during a formal interview. So if you ever find yourself faced with this situation, the best approach is to respond with a question. For instance, in response to a comment about their children, you could ask, 1405 "How old is your son/daughter?" Likewise, in response to any statements relating to health, you could simply state "oh dear, I'm sorry to hear of your knee trouble. How did you hurt it?" These responses maintain a friendly connection, without giving anything away. In most cases, this will be sufficient to move the interview along.

**MISERY LOVES COMPANY**

# The guise
## OF A POSITIVE QUESTION

Lets say that partly through the interview when the recruiter asks how soon you can start. This is a simple question and one that has positive connotations. Unfortunately, this is an example of a trick question, which has been disguised as a positive one. When candidates hear this question, the natural response is one of excitement as they feel they are being offered the job. Without much thought, they begin to express a willingness to get started straight away.

The problem with this response is that if you are in employment your answer indicates that you are not willing to provide appropriate notice, and therefore will not be fulfilling obligations to your current employer. This surely does not work in your favour.

The best answer in response to this question is to affirm, "I have the energy and enthusiasm to start straight away. All I need is two week's notice for my current employer".

# The abrupt end

The abrupt end is just how it sounds. All of the sudden, as if from out of nowhere, the interviewer declares an end to the interview. They show you to the door and thank you for your time. What should you make of this?

This sort of abrupt end is very similar to the silent treatment trick, in the sense that the interviewer is seeking your reaction to the stress of uncertainty. At this point, the formal interview really is over, however, your assessment is not. Your reaction will be observed very closely as you depart from the room and exit the premises. Do you remain composed or do you storm out of the building in defiance? Do you acknowledge the receptionist on your departure or simply ignore them?

As soon as you realise that the interview has reached its conclusion, regardless of what has happened and how you are feeling, it is important to depart gracefully for that final lasting impression.

Gather your belongings and, as you rise from your seat, straighten your clothing. Upon standing, thank the interviewer for his or her time and offer a final handshake. Make your way towards the door, stop and turn, and say your final thank you before making your exit. As you approach the front desk, acknowledge the receptionist with a sincere thank you and continue on your way. Only when you are clear of the area can you let out the scream of defiance, not before.

Does this abrupt end mean that you have been unsuccessful? Absolutely not! In fact, if handled well it could mark your success.

# The telephone
## SCREENING TRAP

In a quest to save time and money, some airlines are now adopting telephone-screening techniques. The telephone screening allows selectors to eliminate unsuitable candidates without going to the expense of inviting them to attend an interview.

As is the case with the interview, this initial telephone screening is laden with tricks and traps. The most cunning of these traps is the time the call takes place. Recruiters will often ring at inopportune times, such as first thing in the morning, on a weekend or during teatime. The reason they do this is because they are hoping to catch the candidate in their natural, and hectic environment. Are there children screaming in the background? Do you answer the telephone in a friendly tone or an unwelcoming one? And if you are caught at a bad time, how do you handle it?

They may also use the friendly recruiter routine to encourage dialogue, the abrupt end and the awkward silence.

Each of which can be extra tricky when you cannot observe their body language or facial expression.

As you cannot predict when the call will come, you should be prepared as soon as you submit a resume or application form. At any time you get an incoming call from an unknown number, take yourself into a quiet room, and be sure to answer in a polite and friendly manner.

If you are caught at an inopportune time, politely ask the caller to hold for a brief moment while you move to a quiet location. Alternatively, if the timing is really bad, you can respectfully request an alternative date and time by saying "I do apologise, but is there a time I can reach you later? I'm very interested in the position and want to give you my undivided attention, but I'm afraid that now isn't the best time."

"If you do what you've always done, you'll get what you've always gotten"

*- Anthony Robbins*

# UNDERCOVER OPERATIONS

# Undercover
## OPERATIONS

It is by no means a secret that candidates rarely show their true selves during a formal interview process. They will do their best to say all the right things, hide undesirable traits and say what they think the recruiters want to hear. After all, it is only natural that you'll want to be seen in the best possible light. The problem is, this makes it extremely difficult for personnel to accurately gage whether any one particular candidate is truly a good fit for the job, the airline and its corporate culture, or is just playing a very good part for the interview.

The task of filtering through hundreds or thousands of applicants is an arduous one and, to make matters worse, there are only a few short hours in which to accomplish it.

To relieve some of this pressure, undercover personnel are often placed among the group during recruitment days. It is these undercover officers who pose the greatest threat to your ultimate success, as their primary objective is to filter and eliminate candidates as quickly as possible, and for any reason they see fit. They are largely accountable for the high percentage of failure rates and are the reason why many candidates leave the interview feeling confused about their elimination.

*"Undercover officers pose the greatest threat to your success"*

# Hidden
## ASSESSMENTS

**From the moment you step foot on the airline's territory, these officers are watching and judging your every move.**

Your personal conduct, how you interact socially and professionally, and the information you reveal, are constantly being scrutinised and assessed. Any mishap or red flags raised during this crucial encounter can land your resume in the rejection pile and you to the nearest exit. There are no second chances.

Within the guise of a fellow candidate, these officers can observe individuals in their relaxed and natural state, and be in a better position to extract information. Unsuspecting candidates openly volunteer information that would never otherwise be revealed, as they are lulled into a false sense of security with seemingly harmless dialogue only to be enticed into mindless gossip and other undesirable behaviours.

During this critical period, officers are observing the reactions of candidates closely as they are encouraged to reciprocate and reveal all sorts of personal and private information. The observations made are then periodically fed back to the recruitment team, who are able to use the information to make informed decisions and better elimination choices in record speed.

# It's not
## WHAT YOU THINK

These officers are not interested in your level of education, previous successes, or best attributes; they are there to uncover information that could potentially cause problems or inconvenience for the airline. As such, the information gathered at this level is not necessarily sized up against the airline's corporate culture and assessment criteria, but rather the hidden criterion and person specification.

It is the information candidates reveal about their health, age, their likes and dislikes, and sensitive information about their background and personal life that are of interest to these officers. Likewise, they will be very interested to learn how you react to certain kinds of behaviours, people and pressures.

Needless to say, a candidate who displays undesirable behaviour or reveal questionable information will not proceed very far.

# Shocking
## REVELATIONS

It never seizes to amaze me how much information unsuspecting candidates will reveal when they think they are not being assessed. In many instances, it isn't even necessary to cajole candidates into confessing information, as many will openly share all sorts of things. Is it really any wonder airlines use undercover personnel?

Here are just some of the revelations I have encountered during my on site excursions.

### Under the influence

"I'm so nervous I think I must have drunk a whole bottle of wine before I arrived."

### Bunking off work

"I had to take a sickie at work just to attend this interview, so it better be worth it."

### Admissions of deceit

"I had to lie on my application just to get invited to this interview"

## Malicious Backbiting

"Did you see what that girl is wearing? What was she thinking?"
"That girl obviously has no brains. I bet she can't even read."

## Negative intentions

"This is such a joke, I wanted to work for . . . but keep failing the damn interview so I have no choice but to apply for this one."
"I just want to work my way into first class so I can meet a rich, good looking guy"

## The hangover

"I'm so hung over from last nights bash, I just want to go to sleep. Wake me when it's over."

## Slandering the boss

"My stupid boss fired me, so I need this job desperately"

Many of these cases are rather extreme, I admit, however, they are by no means rare - I'm sure you've heard similar comments yourself.

As anyone can appreciate, it is these very mindless and irresponsible comments that undercover officers are seeking.

# Innocent
## CASUALTIES

Unfortunately, candidates don't need to be malicious or brash to be excluded from the process. A candidate who innocently mentions their looming personal challenges, such as going through a separation, in a custody battle, recently been made redundant, experiencing financial difficulties, or dealing with a close family member who is in poor health, could raise red flags as to their focus and stability. While such challenges are common and entirely understandable, such circumstances are simply deemed too risky for an airline.

# What to expect?

While the above shock statements were made by actual caniddates, is it possible that such revelations could also be made by the undercover officers themselves as part of their mini assessment? Absolutely. It is precisely this kind of revelation that officers will use to entice a reaction or a reciprocal response. Be mindful, however, because such assessments aren't always this obvious or extreme. Assessments can be covert and very sneaky, so you always need to be on your guard.

Just as new cabin crew hires are put through an intensive training program, so too are undercover officers. These officers are trained in behavioural analysis and psychological profiling and, with this training, they are able to take on a variety of different roles and employ many different tactics. This makes them very effective at blending in and there is little chance that you will ever be able to identify them with any certainty.

The good news is that simply being aware of their presence and being prepared with a strategy will give you an advantage like no other. In fact, your informed knowledge and inability to be culled by their tricks and traps will make you stand out as a top candidate among the crowd.

Even better still, there is much more that you can do, not only to evade their traps, but also turn them into your greatest ally. All that is required is a conscientious and diligent approach.

# Your greatest ally

While it is accurate to say that the purpose of these undercover officers is to expose unsuitable candidates, they also have the power to approve candidates they deem to be exceptional.

If you are able to evade the tricks and traps laid out during this critical process and maintain a friendly, confident, and positive dialogue there will be no reason to pursue you further with trick questions. They will simply move on to another candidate when they are able to remove themselves from your presence. And if you are able to go one step further and create a connection with the officer, not only will you be put forward as a recommendation, but they will actually try to help you to succeed.

So how do you go about impressing these officers?

# Create
## THE RIGHT IMPRESSION

To impress undercover officers, you simply need to treat everyone you meet in the same positive manner. If you are friendly, respectful and supportive towards your fellow candidates, have a positive outlook and are able to demonstrate an enthusiastic attitude towards any activities that you are asked to undertake, the officers will naturally pick up on your positive energy.

Moreover, it is important to remember that anything you say, even in jest or small talk, can and will be used against you. Thus you should avoid volunteering inappropriate information, and your personal life should remain personal.

Naturally this can be easier said than done, so I have devised a line-up of potential scenarios to help you recognise and diffuse any situation you may encounter.

# The Lineup

Undercover officers are like actors. They come in many shapes and sizes and their pseudo personalities are just as diverse. Because you'll never really know whether a candidate is truly a candidate or an undercover officer, it is important that you treat everyone the same. Here is the line-up of the common personalities that you may come across and how to deal with each of them in an appropriate manner.

## The Show-Off

You can be certain to find a show-off at every cabin crew interview. You will recognise him or her by their showy, self-absorbed and obnoxious attitude. While this personality type is easily annoying, the truth is that these individuals tend to be deeply insecure. They brag about their own achievements through fear that nobody will otherwise notice. Be kind and sincerely acknowledge their efforts when appropriate. This will demonstrate that you are not easily antagonised, but are also sensitive to the feelings of others.

## The Rival

In playing the part of the rival, the officer will demonstrate a very competitive streak, which puts you and everyone else as their competition and a threat to their success. They will attempt to make you feel inferior in order to throw you of guard. With these personality types, it is important to be friendly, but respectful of their space. Remember, competitive people are passionate, driven and innovative, so embrace these positive traits and don't let their feeling of superiority run you down.

## The Show-Off

Gossipmongers like to point out other people's flaws or failures in an attempt to feel superior. This personality type is a favourite amongst officers because it can reveal a great deal about a candidate. Are you passive or assertive? Do you engage in gossip or show disapproval?

The best defence in this scenario is to first neutralise the negative comment by pointing out a positive and contrary opinion and then attempting to change the subject. If you have a tenacious officer, they may continue to press. In this instance, it would be wise to respectfully state that you would rather not discuss the merits of others, as it is not your place to do so. This honest approach should dissolve any further discussion on the subject. Failing that, it would be best to take your leave immediately.

## The Think-They-Know-It-All

Know-it-all's have an attitude of superiority and like to think they are experts in everything. In conversation, they are arrogant and condescending and openly disregard the opinion of others. Remain cordial and patient and, whatever you do, don't be drawn into a debate, become critical or impatient. If the so called expert becomes overbearing or it is obvious that they are not an expert at all, you assertiveness skill s may be being tested, so you may tactfully and respectfully state the facts as you perceive them.

## The Overly Anxious

The part of an anxious candidate is a prime opportunity to observe your patience and sensitivity. Experiencing a heightened level of anxiety is very traumatic and paralysing, so be friendly and supportive with these individuals. Offer words of encouragement, but don't place too much focus on their anxiety. Rather, try to break their state by asking questions about things they enjoy and that make them feel relaxed. You could ask them about their hobbies or desires.

## The Negativist

Ah, the negativist. There's always one in every crowd and officers love to use this one to gauge a candidate's ability to remain positive under pressure. At best, negativists are very annoying. At worst, they will drain every ounce of energy and motivation from your body. If your attempts to motivate or encourage these people fall flat, remain positive and try to distance yourself as much as possible. If this is not possible, detach yourself from their words and stay focused on your own positive energy.

## The Aggressor

Passive aggressors are covert and manipulative. They disguise their attacks as constructive criticism or harmless jokes so that, in the instance that they are confronted, they can deny any wrong doing. If you find yourself under attack from these predators, you may ask questions that will temp them into the open, such as: "Forgive me, but that sounded like a disrespectful comment, was it?" In the worst case, you may try to distance yourself.

If the aggressor is more openly disrespectful and disparaging, the best approach is to remain calm and composed, listen attentively and without interruption until they have finished. A counter attack will only reflect badly on you, so resist the tendency to fight back. Instead, acknowledge their opinion and then voice your own in a respectful manner or simply remove yourself from them as much as possible.

## The Open Book

If an individual airs all their dirty laundry to you, revealing all sorts of personal hardships, it could be that they are looking for a reciprocal response. You may demonstrate empathy for their situation, but avoid getting drawn too deeply into conversation about of their hardship and avoid revealing any of your own. Changing the subject and pointing out the positive is always the best course of action.

# The Unusual Suspects

The aforementioned scenarios are rather obvious, so they are generally easier to contend with. Where the traps really lie are in those personalities, which are not negative at all. In fact, it is the positive personalities, such as those in the following scenarios, which will often catch a candidate off guard. Because these personality types are friendly, approachable and easy to get on with, it is very easy to lose yourself in conversation with such individuals. It is with these personality types that you really need to be on your guard. So lets take a look at the contenders.

## The Extrovert

Extroverts are very sociable creatures and thrive on interaction. They are comfortable speaking to large audiences, are very open with their thoughts and feelings, and take an enthusiastic approach to most activities. This personality type is easy to get caught up in dialogue with, so you need to be extra cautious about the information you openly reveal when in their intoxicating presence. Enjoy the buzz they create and allow their enthusiasm to radiate through you and if you have an introverted tendency, just bide you time and make an effort to enjoy their vibrant presence.

## The Entertainer

Just like extroverts, entertainers are sociable, talkative and very energetic people. They love to be the centre of attention and often have an infectious personality. It is very easy to like the entertainer as they have a very down to earth and friendly attitude. When interacting with an entertainer, avoid being overly serious and just allow their positive energy to flow through you. An officer will use this type of personality to lure you into a false sense of security, so beware.

## The Model

In using the term 'model', I am not referring to looks. Rather, I am referring to those candidates who seem to be models of perfection. They appear to say and do all the right things, seemingly without a care or worry in the world. They naturally exude charisma and confidence, and have a magnetic personality. Officers will use this personality type for two reasons. The first is so officers can gauge other candidates reactions to their presence, and two, they will be providing an example for others to learn from. In observing these candidates, examine what makes them appear perfect and be appreciative of those traits.

## The Leader

Natural leaders are instantly recognisable by their innate desire to step up. Their confident, assertive and intelligent character inspires trust in others, while their sensitive, inspiring and sincere side inspires confidence. Officers will often use this approach to test a candidate's ability and willingness to support and encourage their fellow candidates without viewing them as competition. In the presence of a good leader, respect, support and encourage their efforts. Participate and be an active member of their team and you may just join them in the next round.

These are just some of the personality types that you may come across, but there may be many more. So always be on your guard with everyone you come in contact with.

# Handling
## QUESTIONS & DIALOGUE

Handling a personality type is one thing, but answering their intrusive questions or resisting deadly dialogue is quite another. So here are a few tips that will help you in this most critical part of the process.

## Q: So, what do you do for a living?

This question is so common and seemingly innocent that it is easy to get caught out with. If you are between jobs, dislike your current job, or are desperate to find a new job this question can lead to and encourage negative dialogue. When answering this question, just remember to keep the discussion positive and be careful not to reveal too much about your personal circumstances if they are less than ideal.

## Q: Don't you just hate interviews?

Let's be honest, unless you are like me and attend them for fun or research purposes, it is unlikely that you will relish attending interviews. However, just as you would attempt to diffuse a negative interview question with a positive response, you should do the same here. So, rather than admit to disliking interviews, you can state that you simply see it as a necessary part of the process in achieving the job that you desire and, therefore, you appreciate its necessity.

## Q: This is my seventh attempt. How many interviews have you attended?

If an applicant asks you any questions regarding your previous interview attempts or current interview strategies you really must not divulge such information. You could attempt to change the subject in the first instance or, failing that, you may be polite and state that you would rather not focus on the past as you are trying to remain focused on the present.

## Q: I had to take a sickie to attend this damn thing, how did you manage to take time off?

This question has many motives and your best response is a neutral one. Simply state that you have been preparing for this day for some time and have allocated time into your schedule for its purpose. There is no need to say any more.

## Q: I want this job because ... What about you?

An honest and passionate response to this question will surely set you apart, so by all means share this passion if you feel it is appropriate to do so. Clearly the lure of travel is not appropriate, but you may be surprised that some individuals still use this line.

## Q: My daughter decided to misbehave, today of all days. Do you have children?

This question is trying to elicit further information about your personal life. Rather than divulge this personal information you may choose to ignore it and just empathise by saying " Kids sure do pick their moments don't they? But you've got to love them". You may then attempt to change the subject. Asking follow-up questions will only encourage further dialogue and you will want to avoid this where possible.

## Q: Why do we have to sing and dance? Surely this isn't part of our job description

This comment is trying to entice you to speak negatively about a task. This doesn't necessarily have to be about singing and dancing, it could be about any task. Even if you share their viewpoint, remain positive by indicating that you find such challenges fun and are eager to get involved. Nobody will know how you really feel if you don't share it.

# Artful dodging

If you encounter a tenacious officer who continues to press your buttons or if you feel backed into a corner at any time, there may be no alternative but to relieve yourself from their presence as soon as possible.

In planning your escape, you will want to make it as seamless and natural as possible so that you can avoid, or at least minimise, causing offence. You could do this during a task or a session break when the individual is conversing with other candidates. This will make it less likely that your disappearance will be noticed. Whatever you do, be sure to have a plan in mind or you risk being left alone and looking like a lost puppy: This surely won't do you any favours.

Sure there will be a risk that a real candidate may feel insulted or upset if they catch on to your disappearing act, however, if your escape is truly justified, then such candidates are not worthy of your concern as they will only bring you down. On the other hand, an officer will at least recognise your ability to distance yourself from negative situations.

Now that you understand what you are up against, it is time to learn how to make yourself unforgettable...

## MAKE YOURSELF
# UNFORGETTABLE
### PART 2

# Contents
## Of this Session

**5** Polish your appearance

**6** Create the right impression

**7** Create a memorable impression

A strong, positive self image is the best possible preparation for success

*- Joyce Brothers*

# POLISH YOUR APPEARANCE

# Debunking
## THE MYTHS

Before we continue on I feel it is important to address some of the myths that are circulating with regards to appearance.

These myths usually imply that airlines only hire crew who embody perfect figures and harbour model looks. This is, quite frankly, utter nonsense. While there is no denying that airlines require candidates to be well groomed and portray a polished image, this element is usually taken out of context and to the extreme.

For candidates who have been victims of the hidden criteria, and already harbour self-doubts about their appearance, this myth often remains one of the few logical explanations that they can establish. This is often exaggerated further if other attractive candidates are seen to be successful.

Unfortunately, such misconceptions are highly destructive, not only to the candidates who may feel inadequate or self-conscious about their own appearance, but also for those who are blessed with above average appearance. Such candidates are unfairly alienated by candidates who feel intimidated in their presence or, worse still, feel themselves superior, thereby leading them into a false sense of security.

Whatever your appearance concerns, the good news is that there are many simple things you can do to dramatically enhance your outward appearance, and you don't have to resort to surgical intervention.

Okay, now that those myths have been officially debunked, we can press on.

# That all-important
## FIRST IMPRESSION

During the first few minutes of meeting you, the recruitment team will make judgements about your character and suitability based on your overall presentation and appearance. This means that your standard of dress, level of grooming and how you portray yourself through your body language and carriage are all being scrutinised. Therefore, if you are to succeed in creating that all-important positive first impression, it is essential that you make an extra effort to establish a presence.

There is no doubt that appearing professional is the key to creating the best impression at a cabin crew interview. The trouble is, being professional is only part of it. Put a robot into a suit and it too would look professional, but would the robot get the job? It is unlikely.

The fact is, airlines are not looking to hire a suit, but rather they are looking to hire an individual with a personality and character. So why do so many candidates arrive at the interview dressed in the same boring attire? Because it is safe and many are afraid to change the status quo.

Think about it for a moment. How many times have you attended an interview only to be faced with countless other black suits and white shirts? Too many to count I'll bet. Suddenly, that feeling of confidence you had when you set out soon vanishes, leaving you feeling like just another face in the sea of people. If you think it's bad from your point of view, just take a look from the recruiter's perspective.

Establishing a presence is much simpler than many realise, but few ever successfully achieve. Why do so few succeed in this vital area? Because of misunderstandings and misinterpretations.

# Misconceptions
## AND MISINTERPRETATIONS

The only true common denominator for interview attire is the word 'professional'. But what does it actually mean to look professional? Does looking professional indicate that you must wear black or 50 shades of grey? It most certainly does not. Does it mean that you have to dress like clerical admin staff? Heck no. So why do 95% of individuals do just that? Because that is the advice commonly given out by mainstream career advisors.

The trouble with mainstream advice is that it assumes a one-size-fits-all approach, and one size certainly does not fit all. Mainstream advice would have you believe that wearing designer garments or appearing fashionable is too much, that wearing red lipstick is too sexual and wearing any other colour beyond the achromatic range will result in rejection. They even suggest that females de-sexualise themselves in order to appear more professional and authoritative. If you are interviewing for an administrative or managerial post, this 50 shades of grey and the no makeup look may work well, but this is a cabin crew interview and this age old, run-of-the-mill advice simply does not cut it.

Rather than continue to follow this out-dated advice, it is time to make changes. Changes that will no longer leave you looking like everyone else, becoming just another face in the sea of people. Instead, you will establish a presence that gets you noticed for all the right reasons.

It's time to stand out, by not fitting in.

# Stand out
## BY NOT FITTING IN

Dressing in a certain way solely because that is what you think is expected of you Is not the way to stand out. In fact, wearing something that is not conducive to your personality and style will not only make you feel uncomfortable, it will also strip you of your personality. Professional or not, if you are not feeling at your best it will show and you will not be maximising your opportunity.

Now I am not suggesting that you wear a bold red dress or a bright blue suit, and neither am I suggesting that you throw away your black power outfit. What I am suggesting is that you maximise your outfit according to your personal style and confidence level.

If wearing a black suit or achromatic mix makes you feel supremely confident and powerful then that is perfectly fine, but if you are only wearing this type of outfit for the sake of keeping up appearances, it is unlikely that you will feel comfortable and unable to function at your best.

Ultimately the best outfit to wear is the one that you feel the most comfortable and confident in. Clearly there are some limits and guidelines that need to be observed, however, if you feel at your best in what you are wearing, your aura will shine through and that is what will make you memorable.

Now before you dash off to the nearest shopping mall to purchase that fab outfit that I know you've had your eye on, take heed and consider the following important guidelines.

# Style Guide:

## LADIES

### Consider: Style

Presence is achieved when you look and feel good, so it is important to wear an outfit that you feel the most confident and powerful in. However, in order to stand out for the right reasons, it is important to achieve balance: Balance between how the outfit makes you feel and what impression it creates.

Your outfit should be thoughtful and demonstrate that you have made an effort. So buy the best quality garnets that you can afford, and be sure they are clean and neatly pressed. The idea is to look business-like, yet stylish.

Tasteful, elegant and sophisticated are good objectives to aim for, and you'll want to avoid appearing flashy or overly sexy. Well-coordinated and tailored separates achieve this perfectly, as does a fitted dress in a conservative style: Conservative implying a modest neckline and appropriate length. A quality tailored jacket is a powerful piece that can tie a look together and create a streamlined and professional appearance.

Avoid heavy patterns, as these can appear overwhelming, and be sure to select wrinkle resistant fabrics, such as wool. Nothing looks more unprofessional or unprepared than rumpled clothes or wrinkled shirts.

## Consider: Colour

Colour is a powerful tool that can dramatically increase your chances of standing out. Used appropriately, colour will help you to convey confidence, express your personality and enhance your complexion. So, consider adding a splash of your favourite colour to your outfit for added pizazz.

How much colour you wear will depend on you. There is not necessarily anything wrong with wearing a red pencil dress provided you have the strength of character to pull it off and the colour is flattering against your complexion. However, such a bold statement piece should not be underestimated and must be worn with caution. If you choose to wear a bold piece, be sure that you have the courage of your convictions because you will certainly be noticed and expectations will be set much higher. You wouldn't want to be noticed for looking extremely uncomfortable or for looking washed out by an unflattering colour.

You don't need to be draped in colour to make an impact. In fact, the safest way to wear colour is to add subtle splashes through your accessories, accents or pop pieces. Subtle accents can bring out the sparkle in your eyes and liven up your outfit, without appearing overwhelming or degrading your professionalism.

Whatever you ultimately decide, a contrasting style will bring a sense of balance to the outfit. For a bold and striking colour, opt for a very conservative cut and for a pale tint, add life by selecting a striking style..

## Consider: Shoes

The benefits of wearing heels are obvious. They make your legs look longer, shapelier and more feminine, so it is a good idea to wear them if you feel comfortable to do so. Killer heels may have the added butt lifting effect, however, this is not the look you want to achieve at an interview. Heels should be no higher than 3" and thin soles will appear more professional and elegant than thick platforms.

For those of you who are not used to wearing heels or are on the taller side, 1" inch heels will still provide the benefits of wearing heels without the excess height.

Only wear shoes which are clean and in good condition. Tatty shoes, with scuffed toes or heels will detract from the polished image you are trying to create. Open toes, sling backs and splashes of colour are perfectly acceptable as long as they are tasteful and not overly sexy or decorative fashion styles.

## 🔸 Consider: Hosiery

If wearing a dress or a skirt, pantyhose in plain nude or black are essential for creating a polished and professional image, as they will ensure your legs look perfectly smooth and blemish free. Be sure to select a good quality pair, as they will hug your curves better than cheaper alternatives and will be less likely to create the unsightly wrinkled effect around the knees and ankles. Be sure to spot check them before the interview to ensure that there are no runs or ladders and always have an emergency pair in your handbag for good measure.

## 🔸 Consider: Accessories

Jewellery is a great way to spice up a boring black ensemble, giving it character and pizazz, however, be sure to keep your pieces minimal and conservative. Wear no more than one ring per hand, and one set of earrings, and avoid oversized fashion pieces. Bangles that clink can become distracting and annoying, so it is best to avoid them. A timepiece can be worn, but be sure the style is appropriate and turn off any audible sounds.

Observe caution when wearing an engagement ring or wedding band, as such pieces will draw attention to your private life and will leave you open to discrimination.

## Consider: Grooming

Grooming is an essential aspect when presenting a polished image. They are the finishing touches that tie your appearance together. Bitten nails, unsightly blemishes and scruffy hair can undermine even the very best of outfits. So be sure to pay extra special attention to the following areas:

Nails should be clean, neatly trimmed and reasonable in length. Nail polish should match in colour and it is best to avoid charms, glitter and multi-coloured polish.

Use cosmetics to conceal blemishes and enhance your assets, but avoid going over the top. Tastefully applied makeup is the best way to achieve a polished and sophisticated look. A touch of mascara and some eyeliner paired with a dash of lipstick is all that is needed. Remember, you are attending an interview not going out for a night on the town. Refined elegance will work better than dramatic.

**Tip**: Red lipstick is a favourite among most airlines so wearing it to the interview is a fantastic psychological finishing touch. Be sure to visit a cosmetics counter to find the ideal shade of red for your complexion. The wrong shade will be noticeable as it will wash you out and ruin the effect.

Hair should be neat and well groomed, and outrageous colours or styles should be avoided. Frizzy or loose ends can appear messy so brush and fix them into place if necessary. Freshly trimmed hair will be easier to style and keep looking fresh, so book into the salon if necessary.

If you choose to wear perfume, select a light scent and wear it sparingly. There is nothing more off-putting than an overpowering odour, even a pleasant one.

Visible tattoos and facial piercings are not acceptable. Tattoos will need to be concealed and piercings removed. That applies to multiple earrings too.

# Consider: The ultimate advantage

Interviewers need to be able to visualise you in the position, so the very act of looking like you are already cabin crew will create a great psychological advantage.

Now, I am not implying that you find a suit in a matching colour to the airlines' uniform with hat and scarf to match. Sure this would make you stand out, but not for the right reasons. Subtlety is the key to success with this strategy. You're trying to capture the airlines aesthetic appeal, not look like you are attending a fancy dress parade.

The best way to pull this off is to look at the cabin crew who already work for the airline. Is red lipstick a part of the uniform? What are the typical hair grooming styles? Are their corporate colours muted, pale or bold? And what about the corporate culture? Is the airline energetic, carefree and fun loving, or conservative and professional? Understanding these aspects will help you to achieve the most appropriate interview look for each airline.

Injecting a splash of the corporate colour into your accessories is a great touch. Another is to tend to your grooming in the same way you would if offered the position. Understanding the corporate culture will further enable you to tailor your outfit according to the tastes of the airline. If the airline is famous for its fun and carefree corporate culture, you can be sure they will be more accepting of bold colours and unique styling, whereas an airline known for its conservative image may not be.

The effort you put in to this will show and it will be apparent that you have done your research to understand the airline's culture. The psychological impact this one trick can achieve is astonishing and should not be underestimated.

## Avoid: Fashion faux pas

If you would like to be taken seriously, you need to avoid the following fatal mistakes.

1. Push up bra and plunging necklines

2. Bare midriff

3. Too much makeup or hair product

4. Unnecessary accessories

5. Wrinkled or unkempt clothes

6. Ill fitting garments

7. Cheap and translucent blouses

8. Scuffed or tatty shoes

9. Short skirt

10. Extremely high heels or large platforms

11. Bitten or over the top nails

12. Strong perfume

# Style Guide:
## GENTS

When it comes to looking professional, the options for gents are no doubt limited. Formal business attire is essential for creating a professional, polished and streamlined look, however, when every other male candidate is also wearing business attire, how do you stand out from the crowd? It is the attention you pay to the finer details that will show that you have made an effort, and it is this that will get you noticed.

## Consider: Fit & Quality

The key to looking your best in a suit is to pay special attention to fit and quality. A well-tailored suit, in a wrinkle free fabric, will create a polished and professional look that will surely set you apart from the rest. Off the rack suits are a popular choice because they are convenient and inexpensive, however, a ready to wear suit is often the worst option when making a good impression is your top priority. As such, it is advisable to purchase the best quality suit you can afford. A custom tailored suit is the obvious choice, however if finances will not stretch to this, purchase an off the rack suit and have some tailored alterations carried out for an inexpensive alternative.

Whichever option you choose, be sure to pay attention to selecting a good quality fabric. Natural fabrics are far better than synthetic fabrics or blends. In particular, wool, such as merino, cashmere and angora, will offer the best in comfort, wrinkle resistance, and longevity.

## Consider: Shirt

A good quality, 100% cotton shirt, with long sleeves is essential for appearing professional and crisp. White, ecru and blue are classic and conservative choices and should be your first choice.

Dark shirts are somewhat taboo as they are often considered a style choice, rather than a professional one. As such, you need to proceed with caution if this is what you feel most comfortable wearing. On the one hand it is important to wear what you feel confident and powerful in, but on the other, it is important to achieve balance: Balance between how the outfit makes you feel and what impression it creates. Airlines are no doubt much more open to personal style choices, however, it is a choice that may not be viewed favourably, no matter how powerful and confident it makes you feel. Therefore, it is far better to play it safe.

When it comes to choosing a collar, remember that it will frame your face. As such, you will want to select a collar that brings balance to your face shape. A wide spread collar will compliment a thin and long face well, while a classic point works better on a round face.

## Consider: Pattern & Colour

With regards to colour and pattern, it is best to err on the side of caution. Traditional colours, such as navy blue or charcoal grey, are great alternatives to the standard black, while brown, beige and taupe will appear too casual. If you do decide to wear black, try opting for a subtle pinstripe pattern to break up the monotony and strength of the colour.

## Consider: Tie

The tie is an extremely important accessory, as it is often the first thing that a person notices.

Since it frames your face, it is important to consider the colour choice carefully because the wrong colour can suck the sparkle out of your complexion, leaving you looking dull and lifeless. When considering colour, assess how it interacts and enhances your complexion. Does red make your skin look bright, vibrant and well rested? or does it make you look sallow and washed out? Likewise, does blue bring a sparkle to your eyes, or does it make your complexion look muddy and ashen?

Pattern is another factor that needs consideration. Character ties and exotic patterns, while demonstrating personality, are not the ideal interview choice. Instead, opt for subtle stripes, simple designs or block colours for a classic and professional look.

For a strong and confident appeal opt for a larger knot, such as the Pratt or Windsor and aim for a length that falls to the same level as the belt buckle. Tie bars and clips may also be worn to keep the tie in place.

## Consider: Shoes & Socks

Shoes should be worn in a style and colour that coordinates with the overall look of your suit. Lace up shoes are the classic and safe option, however, loafers can also be worn if they are suitable. A thin sole will create a more professional image than thick rubber soles.

Nicked heels and scruffy toes will ruin the whole outfit, so invest in a new pair if necessary and never underestimate the importance of a good shoeshine.

Socks should be inconspicuous so they don't draw any attention. As such, they should be dark in colour and long enough to cover your calves so that your flesh is not exposed when seated.

## Consider: Accessories

Accessories are finishing touches and should be treated as such. This means that they should remain simple to complement your outfit. Cufflinks may be worn if you are wearing a buttonless shirt, and a leather belt with an understated buckle ought not be forgotten.

While a leather briefcase is unnecessary, a leather portfolio will look much more professional than carrying lots of loose papers.

When it comes to jewellery, the simpler and less of it, the better. One ring and a tasteful wristwatch is all that is necessary to project a professional image.

## Consider: Grooming

When it comes to grooming a good haircut and clean-shaven face are essential. A few days prior to the interview, have your hair freshly cut or trimmed and be sure to shave on the morning of the interview. Be careful not to cut yourself and try to prevent razor burn.

Nails are another aspect that is often neglected and underestimated by male candidates. A manicure is an attention to detail that will be noticed and appreciated, so visit a manicurist a few days before the interview.

If you must wear cologne, be sure not to use too much as it can be distracting and suffocating.

## Consider: The Ultimate Advantage

Interviewers need to be able to visualise you in the position, so the very act of looking like you are already cabin crew will create a great psychological advantage. Now, I am not implying that you arrive in something too similar to the airlines' uniform; however, it doesn't hurt to capture an element of the industries aesthetic appeal. The one item that captures this look the best is a fitted waistcoat. It is an element often under-utilised, but its stylish appeal works wonders within the airline industry.

Some of you may baulk at this idea, however, it is an element, which will get you noticed. Not only do they create a business-like and streamlined appearance, but it will show that you have made an extra special effort. Take a look at the Virgin Atlantic uniform to get a sense of its style for yourself. If a waistcoat does fit in with your personal style, consider including it in your repertoire.

## ⚠ Avoid: Fashion Faux Pas

If you would like to be taken seriously, you need to avoid the following fatal mistakes.

1. Short sleeves

2. Strong cologne

3. Too much hair product

4. Excessive jewellery

5. Wrinkled or unkempt clothes

6. Ill fitting garments

7. Scuffed or tatty shoes

8. Visible tattoos or piercings

9. Rubber sports watch

10. Bow tie or suspenders

11. Excessive facial hair

# Appearance
## CONCERNS

With all the guidance provided and even some myths debunked, I know there are still some of you who have concerns over your appearance. So let's address this before we continue forward.

For those of you with minor or temporary imperfections, such as the occasional pimple or patch of dry skin, I understand that a spot in the middle of your forehead is not ideal, but it isn't a disaster either. Recruiters are human too and will recognise that this is a temporary imperfection and will not base a hiring decision upon it. Likewise if you have a perceived flaw, such as an unusual face shape, off white teeth or a slightly crooked nose, these are characteristics that make you unique and are highly unlikely to make any sort of impact to the strength of your candidacy. So please stop worrying about extremes and focus your attention on what really matters.

On the other hand, if you do have a real concern, such as rosacea, acne, birthmarks or severely stained teeth, it is unfortunate that such appearance concerns can be cause for discrimination, so it really is worthwhile looking into treatments that may be available to you. With the advances in technology, it would appear that nothing is beyond fixing these days, so there is usually a treatment that will work for you.

For scaring, there are non-evasive laser procedures that can drastically minimise their appearance and for acne, there is medication and lotions. For rosacea, dark circles or birthmarks, you will find medical strength concealers and for stained teeth, cosmetic dentistry or tooth whitening procedures. Whatever path you ultimately decide to pursue, it is important to proceed with safety and due consideration.

## In Conclusion

While the advice and guidance given in this chapter may sound obvious, unnecessary and, even, unimportant, it has been my experience that many candidates fail to create an impression because they are either confused or uninformed about the standard of dress expected of them or because they neglect to pay enough attention to the details.

Following this guidance will not only multiply your chances of attracting the interviewers attention, but you will also stand out for having made an extra effort.

In the grand scheme of things, it does not matter how well you are dressed or how much effort you have gone through if the rest of your delivery is poor. So, continue reading and you will discover important steps that will make you truly memorable.

> You can't depend on your eyes when your imagination is out of focus
>
> *- Mark Twain*

# CREATE THE
# RIGHT
## IMPRESSION

# Consider
## YOUR COMMUNICATION

Because effective communication skills are essential for interview success, it is important to be mindful of how your communication is received. This means that you must consider not only the words you use, but also how your tonality and body language complement or contradict those words.

Consider the following communication guidelines:

## Word choice

Words are important because they communicate and convey your message succinctly. So, even at a low 7% accountability, your word choice can mean the difference between a powerful, captivating and influential exchange, and a weak, disempowering and ineffective one.

### Action words

Action words are positive, powerful and directive, and should be used abundantly. Action words include: Communicated, conveyed, directed, listened, persuaded, arranged, handled and improved.

### Filler words

Filler words are useless and annoying verbal mannerisms such as "you know," "huh," "erm," "kind of," "ummm," and "uh". Besides sounding unprofessional, they also distract attention from the message. Filler words should be avoided at all costs.

### Undermining words

Words and phrases such as 'I think,' 'I hope,' 'maybe,' 'sort of,' 'perhaps,' 'I guess,' all undermine your message and credibility by creating the impression that you don't trust your own knowledge or opinion. Eliminating these phrases will drastically improve the quality of any message.

### Jargon, slang and cliches

Specialist terminology and informal expressions can confuse an outside audience. Avoid these where possible, and stick to simple, clear and coherent language.

## Vocal quality

Tonality plays a key role in sending the correct messages. So, if your aim is to project confidence, enthusiasm and expertise, it is important to exercise control and awareness of your tonality throughout your interactions.

## Pitch

Pitch refers to the degree of highness and lowness in your voice. A variation in your pitch creates meaning, adds clarity and makes what you are saying more interesting. For instance: A rise in your pitch suggests you are asking a question, which indicates doubt, uncertainty and hesitation. A fall in pitch indicates a statement, which suggests certainty and assurance.

## Tempo

Tempo refers to the speed of your voice. If you speak too slowly, you risk losing the interest and attention of your audience. If you speak too fast, others may find you difficult to follow. The key is to maintain a pace, which is fast enough to maintain interest, yet slow enough to be clear.

## Volume

Speaking in a loud volume suggests aggression, while a quiet volume indicates shyness and makes it difficult to be heard. The key to determining the appropriate volume is to keep your voice loud enough to be heard, but soft enough to be clear. Modulation of volume can also be introduced to keep your speech interesting and add extra emphasis.

## Articulation

Articulation refers to vocal clarity. Regardless of our pitch, tempo, volume and accent, you need to make a conscious effort to enunciate clearly.

# Communication Barriers

Barriers to effective communication may arise for a number of reasons. When these barriers do occur, you are forced to become even more effective in your ability to communicate. The strategies below will help overcome some of these more effectively.

## Language

If you struggle with the native language of the airline, or have a very strong accent, speak slowly and clearly, ask for clarification and check for understanding, avoid idioms and jargon, use gestures and be specific, listen actively and be patient.

## Cultural

Because every culture has its own set of values, beliefs and behaviours, the potential for confusion and misunderstanding is high. Even when we speak the same language, these differences can lead to challenges. To effectively connect with an individual from a culturally different background, it is important to be sensitive and respectful, avoid prejudice and stereotyping, and be aware of using questionable language and gestures.

## Gender

Barriers in communication between genders exist primarily because men and women have different communication patterns. To overcome these barriers, it is important to appreciate, learn and understand the different strengths and styles that exist.

While men tend to be more direct and factual, women tend to be indirect and tactful. Men have a preference for reason and logic, are competitive and are interested in power, rank and status. Women are empathetic and feeling oriented. They value relationships and like to build rapport. Men communicate to exchange information and solve problems, while women communicate to share and a build connection.

## Emotional

Emotional barriers within an interview situation manifest themselves through fear, shyness or restraint. When we feel distracted by these emotional states, our ability to communicate at an effective level is severely inhibited. We may wrongly interpret the actions and words of others, and may not effectively express our own opinion. We may even stop listening to the other person as our internal dialogue takes over.

To effectively deal with these barriers, it is important to treat the underlying cause of such emotions.

# Let your body
## DO THE TALKING

The way you carry yourself, the gestures you use and your facial expressions communicate all sorts of messages. If you appear to lack confidence, seem evasive, or exhibit negative body language it is only natural that the interviewer will want to dig further to find out why your body is contradicting your words. So it is worth learning to control certain aspects so that you can convey the message of a well-balanced, confident individual.

The reason why your body language is so important is that it supports and reinforces what you say. In essence you appear to be exactly what you say you are.

## Gestures

We use open gestures when we are feeling confident and relaxed, and are being honest and sincere, therefore, keep your arms unfolded, your legs uncrossed and your palms open. Sitting or standing with your arms crossed will be interpreted as a defensive posture and will give the impression that you are uncomfortable, bored, or have something to hide. Likewise, standing in your hands in your pockets suggests unease.

Touching your nose during the interview is commonly interpreted as an indication of dishonesty, so even if it itches, it is best to grin and bear it. Observe caution if you experience the tendency to rub your neck as this too can be misinterpreted as boredom or unease.

Gesturing can be useful for adding emphasis to what you are saying and, if the movements you employ are subtle and controlled, it is perfectly okay to use gestures to express yourself and endorse your words. For best results, keep any movements below shoulder level, but above the waistline.

## Posture

Posture is fundamental to appearing alert, confident and motivated, and yet it is shocking to see how many candidates forget this one simple rule. Take a look around the room next time you attend a group interview and you will see candidates slouching and generally looking bored and inattentive while they wait to be assessed.

I understand that the wait can be long and tiresome, however, it is important that you do not let this happen to you. This is the period when you are being watched very closely and letting your posture relax too much will demonstrate disrespect and give the impression that you lack interest.

To portray the image of a confident and motivated person, adopt an upright and attentive posture that is open, yet relaxed. Keep your chin parallel to the floor, shoulders back and spine straight.

If seated, lean slightly forward with your hands loosely in your lap, or on the table. Place both feet flat on the floor, or cross your ankles. And always be sure to direct your body and your feet towards the interviewer and not at the door, as this will give the impression that you feel uncomfortable and are ready to flee.

If standing, keep your arms loosely at your side or behind your back and plant your feet about 8-10 inches apart. If standing for long periods, place one foot slightly in front of the other to allow you to smoothly and unnoticeably shift weight between your feet.

## Your carriage

The way you carry yourself is a powerful indicator of how you feel. To be perceived as confident and professional, walk briskly with an erect posture. Keep your shoulders back, your arms loosely at your side, and chin parallel to the floor.

## Facial expressions

Your facial expressions convey a wide range of attitudes, feelings and emotions, and these can have a significant impact on your ability to connect with others. Because of this, it is important to be aware of the story your face is telling and work to convey an attentive, sincere and interested expression.

A positive expression can certainly include a smile, but doesn't necessarily imply its inclusion. In fact, maintaining a constant smile is not only uncomfortable, but it is also completely unnecessary. Instead, an open expression that includes a gentle and understated smile, soft eyes and slightly elevated eyebrows will result in a soft and pleasant expression.

Large smiles should be reserved for introductions and the occasional injection during conversation.

## Handshake

Your handshake says a lot about you. A firm handshake conveys confidence, assertiveness and professionalism while a weak, limp handshake suggests shyness and insecurity. A strong, crushing handshake indicates aggression and dominance, and should be avoided.

To perform a professional and confident handshake, follow these simple guidelines:

Before connecting for the handshake establish eye contact, smile and lean slightly forward. As you extend your right hand, keep your hand straight and thumb pointing upwards. When your hands connect engage a firm, but not crushing, grip. Pump one to three times, for a duration of 1-3 seconds, and break away.

# The Eyes
## DEFINITELY HAVE IT

Good eye contact is one of the most important factors of body language. Shifty eyes, or complete avoidance of contact can suggest dishonesty, boredom, rudeness, insecurity or shyness.

If you find eye contact anxiety provoking and uncomfortable, direct your gaze at their eyebrows, forehead, or bridge of the nose. This is not a permanent solution by any means, but it will certainly ease you into the process.

In an attempt to forge eye contact, be aware not to stare as this can indicate aggression and make others feel uncomfortable. To avoid this extreme, lighten your gaze and keep it friendly. This can be achieved by allowing your eyes to go slightly out of focus.

If you have notes, you can temporarily break eye contact as you refer to these, and if there is a second recruitment officer present, this will give you opportunity to break eye contact as you periodically direct your focus back and forth between the two.

Aim to maintain eye contact for 80-90% of the time.

# Caution:
## SMOKERS

Due to the non-smoking environment on board an aircraft and the fact that you will not be able to step outside for a quickie mid-flight, many airlines now have a strict no smoking policy and will not hire smokers. So if you are partial to a cigarette or two, it is important that you refrain from 'sparking up' at any time before or during the interview, as the smell of smoke will linger on your clothing. Once the interview is over, you may of course have one, but be sure you are well away from the building.

To avoid your interview garments becoming infested by the smell of stale smoke, have your outfit cleaned thoroughly and then keep it zipped up in a suit bag away from your smoking environment. On the day of your interview, be sure to wash thoroughly before you handle it.

Although it is possible to try to conceal the smell of smoke, the effort required and the risks involved are far too great and it simply isn't worth it. The best course of action on the day of the interview is to wear a nicotine patch.

If you find the thought of not smoking for the day too much to bear, temporarily switch over to e-cigarettes, but be sure to use it only within the privacy of the W.C. and never in public view.

So, what should you say if you are asked whether you smoke? Well, this will depend on you. You can of course say no, you could be tactful with the truth and simply state that you have recently given up or you can respond in the affirmative. Whichever answer you choose is your decision, but beware that being honest in this instance may be the quickest way for your resume to hit the rejection pile.

In fact, you will find that many airlines now have this as part of the employment contract, so it is worthwhile considering kicking the addiction in the long term.

" I influence anybody who is able to get through the chaos of my first impression. "

*- Gary Vaynerchuck*

# CREATE A
# MEMORABLE
## IMPRESSION

# Create a
## MEMORABLE IMPRESSION

When faced with hundreds, and possibly thousands, of other candidates, merely creating a good impression just isn't enough. You need to be memorable. The trouble is, very few people know how to truly differentiate themselves from the competition. Most candidates enter the interview in their own little bubble, thinking that they only need to dress well and sell their skills and experience. Unfortunately, this is only a small part of it.

Creating a memorable impression goes far beyond what you wear and how you carry yourself, and even beyond the skills and experience you posses. In fact, it is so rare that only 2% of candidates ever make it through to being hired.

The secret to creating a memorable impression will surprise you in its simplicity, and yet many candidates are unaware that such an advantage even exists, let alone know how to evoke it. They often enter the process only prepared for the hard sell, if they are prepared at all, and end up merely blending in with the rest of the crowd.

Recruiters see this same thing time and time again, so any candidate who is prepared to put in just that little bit of extra effort will naturally stand out, and it is these candidates who, ultimately, get hired.

So what is this mysterious phenomenon and how can you use it to your advantage?

# The Art
## OF THE CONNECTION

This technique is actually not mysterious at all. In fact, it is not even a secret. The technique involves creating a connection or, most commonly referred to as, establishing a rapport. Rapport is such a powerful tool, as it is the quickest way to achieve a sensation of familiarity and trust between you and the recruiter. It is so powerful, in fact, that it can even sway the hiring decision in your favour.

Why does this technique work so well? Have you ever met someone for the first time and yet you felt a strong connection, just as if you'd known him or her forever? This is rapport in action. If you can establish this level of rapport with the recruiter or undercover officers, you can be sure they will remember you favourably.

The quickest and easiest way to achieve a connection this strong is through the act of mirroring.

# Mirror, Mirror

Mirroring is a process whereby you match your communication style, posture and mannerisms to those of another person. It is something you do naturally when you are deep in rapport with another person and is created by a deep feeling of unity. Using it consciously can evoke the sensation that the two of you are very much in sync just as readily as if it had occurred at a subconscious level, only you can be in control and use it to your own advantage.

As a note of caution, mirroring is something that must be done subtly to be effective. As such, it is important not to match every movement and not to react instantly to every change, else your motives will become obvious and the effectiveness of the technique will be lost.

For seamless results, take note of the following guidelines.

# Body Language

As you are speaking with the recruiter, make a mental note of how they are sitting or standing, and what they are doing with their hands. Then, subtly mirror their position and gestures. If they are leaning forward, you might lean forward also. If they have their hands clasped on the table, you might do the same.

The best time to mirror a position is when you engage in dialogue. For example: The recruiter leans forward as he or she begins to ask you a question. As you engage in your follow up response, a change in position would appear natural and go completely unnoticed.

Be cautious not to mirror any closed signals, such as crossing your arms, as this will only accomplish a negative connection.

# Communication Style

Mirroring a communication style can be done through using similar words or phrases, matching the sensory style, or mimicking the pitch, tempo and volume of their voice.

**Words and Phrases**
You can make a fantastic psychological impact simply by injecting the recruiter's own terminology and sequence of words into your answers. For example, if the interviewer points out that they are looking for and value a candidate who is 'team spirited', inject the same phrase into your answer. Simply stating that "I work well in a team", or "I am a team player", while implying the same values, will not create the same strong psychological impact as using the interviewers own words.

### Pitch, Tempo and Volume
Matching your pitch, tempo and volume to the recruiters speaking style will make you appear in tune to what they are saying. This will speed up the rapport process and greatly improve your chances of creating a favourable impression. Keep pace with the interviewer and assess their basic conversational style. If they have a fast pace, assume the same characteristics. If they are analytical and introspective, slow down your responses to their speed.

### Sensory Style
While we all use a mix of the sensory styles: Visual, kinaesthetic and auditory, we tend to have a dominant style that we gravitate towards. If, during the course of the interview, it becomes obvious that the recruiter has a preference towards a particular sensory style, you can adjust your style accordingly to establish a deeper connection.

Visual people use words that reflect their visual style, such as: 'I <u>see</u> what you mean', 'It <u>looks</u> to me like...', 'I <u>imagine</u> that...'

Auditory people use hearing words, such as: 'I <u>hear</u> what you are saying', 'We'll <u>discuss</u> this further', 'I <u>hear</u> you loud and clear'

Kinaesthetic people use action words, such as: 'It <u>feels</u> as if...', 'It <u>slipped</u> my mind', 'I have a solid <u>grasp</u>...'

---

Next time you are in a public place, observe how people who appear to be closely connected do these same things. You could even try this out for yourself next time you are out for lunch with a close friend or family member. In fact, because this technique can appear uncomfortable and awkward the first time you try it, practicing will, in time, make it almost natural and automatic, and you may even find that your relationships begin to blossom more than usual.

# Leading

Leading is an influencing technique that can be used to judge the level of connection. For example: If you feel you have achieved rapport with the recruiter, you could change position or make a gesture to see If the recruiter follows your lead. If this does occur, you can be sure that you have established a strong connection. It the test reveals that the connection is not as strong as you thought, simply go back to mirroring to re-establish and strengthen the connection.

# Disconnection

It is important to be perceptive to signs that the recruiter has become disconnected so that you can be proactive in re-establishing the connection.

Before attempting to reconnect, however, it is important to establish the accuracy of your perceptions because you may have simply misread the signal or it could be a by-product of a paranoid imagination. Similarly, the perceived signal may be a momentary motion that has no substance or it may be unrelated to you entirely.

To reliably determine the accuracy of your observation, you first need to scan for clusters of signals that are supportive of your perception. If you observe two or more congruent signals, this is a definite cluster. Next, you can test our connection by attempting to 'lead' (see above). If the recruiter doesn't follow, this is also a sure sign that a disconnection has taken place.

# When to use it

During the group stages, you will not have an opportunity to forge any kind of connection with the official recruiters, however, you will be up close and very personal with the undercover team and it is here that you will be focusing much of your attention during these early stages.

The trouble is, how do you know who is undercover and who is a candidate? Unfortunately ,you don't. As such, the only possible way to accomplish this task is to make this same effort with every candidate you meet. While this may seem like an arduous and inefficient task, your efforts will pay off many times over, as you will gain an advantage like no other. In the worst instance, you will come away with a few new friends.

During the latter stages of the final interview, you can refocus your efforts on the official recruiters. This is where the technique will really come into its own and you can use it to its full advantage.

# The one type
## WHO ALWAYS GETS THE JOB OFFER

As you can now see, there is always one type who gets the job offer, but it isn't the best looking one as myths and legend would have you believe. The simple truth is that recruiters hire those individuals that they personally like and feel a connection with.

The biggest mistake most candidates make is that they enter the interview focused only on themselves and miss any opportunity to make a connection. A candidate who makes an effort will not only come across as more genuine and sincere, they will also instantly differentiate themselves from the competition, so it is certainly worthwhile putting the extra effort into perfecting this technique.

*You're Hired!*

# Just like
## OLD FRIENDS

Another trick, which can be used as an adjunct to the previous technique, is to think of the recruiter as a good friend. Now I am not suggesting you take this literally, or you risk appearing too informal and familiar, what I am suggesting is that you enter the interview in a natural and conversational frame of mind.

The point of this technique is to help you relax, but also to assist the interviewer in breaking the ice. Simply initiating some friendly dialogue as you first meet the recruiter will help you to create an aura of a warm and approachable person, but also one who is relaxed and confident. Such a personable approach can help the interviewer feel more comfortable in your presence and will certainly get the interview off to a great start.

Naturally you will want to use common sense here to avoid stepping over the invisible line, however, it is important to remember that most candidates will only be thinking about themselves. The interviewer will appreciate your effort to connect.

# The enthusiastic APPROACH

If there is just one more thing that can set one candidate apart from the rest, it is the expression of a sincere passion and enthusiasm for the job, airline and the opportunity. Sadly, many people believe that showing enthusiasm will be mistaken for desperation and, as such, suppress their enthusiasm in favour of the laid back and relaxed approach. The truth is, the laid back approach is often mistaken for indifference or disinterest, and this can severely hinder your chances of success.

Another misconception is that being enthusiastic means that you need to be loaded with energy and bouncing off the walls. This is bordering on excitement, rather than enthusiasm, and is not ideal either. As discussed previously, the idea is to match the tempo of the person you are speaking to, and injecting too much energy can make it difficult for others to relate and connect with you, not to mention exhausting. You can certainly be calm and still be enthusiastic.

So what exactly is enthusiasm and how can you use it appropriately?

## Use it appropriately

There are several ways that you can display your enthusiasm. This could be through an eagerness and willingness to learn, your facial expression and smile, an expression of pride in your work, actively listening and asking questions, taking notes and even through your knowledge and research about the opportunity and the airline.

You can also be upfront about your enthusiasm by stating it directly. For instance, when asked "Why do you want to be cabin crew?", speak from the heart as you tell them your personal story and the steps you have been taking to achieve your dream. If you have a sincere passion for meeting people from different cultures, express it. If you have a genuine love for assisting in the comfort of others, use it. If you have been participating in volunteer work to enhance your skills for the position, tell them. This is truly where you will stand head over heels above the run-of-the-mill answers that they hear 95% of the time.

## Don't underestimate the power

It sounds simple, and even, superfluous, when compared to tangible skills and experiences, however, do not underestimate the power of honest and sincere enthusiasm. It is contagious and will energise those around you. More importantly, recruiters will pick up on your positive energy and will sense that you will approach the job with vigour.

# SURVIVAL 101
## PART 3

# Contents
## Of this Session

**8** Resolve common concerns

**9** Manage your nerves

**10** Bloopers, blunders & faux pas recovery

One important key to success is self-confidence. An important key to self-confidence is preparation.

*- Arthur Ashe*

# RESOLVE COMMON CONCERNS

## COMMON CONCERNS

### Challenge: Blushing

**Go green**
A purposeful green-pigmented concealer or foundation will minimise the impact of redness.

**Seek medical advice**
Blushing which is caused by a medical condition should be treated by a medical professional. Prescription medication may be prescribed.

### Challenge: Cottonmouth

Cottonmouth is a natural and protective barrier, which is often caused by nerves. To minimise the effects, be sure to keep fully hydrated on the run up to the event. Fill up on water during breaks and periodically sip on water throughout the assessment.

You can stimulate saliva flow by adding a splash of lemon juice to your water bottle, sucking on sugar free candy or chewing sugarless gum. Gently biting your tongue can also activate the glands that stimulate saliva flow.

Avoid salty and sugary foods, alcohol (including alcohol based mouthwash), caffeinated beverages and tobacco products as these inhibit saliva flow and dry the mouth out further.

## Challenge: Excessive sweating

**Dress Colours**
Black, navy and pure white will help disguise sweat marks, as will the camouflaging nature of patterns. Avoid: Light colours such as pale blue or grey.

**Dress Fabrics**
Wear breathable fabrics such as: 100% cotton, pima cotton, seersucker, linen, 100% wool, merino, and cashmere. Avoid: Corduroy, flannel, silk, polyester and polyester blends, nylon, and acetate

**Dress Style**
Wear loose fitting over and under garments for maximum airflow. Add layers, such as a suit jacket, waistcoat or cardigan, to disguise sweating.

**Medicated Antiperspirant**
Heavy duty, medicated antiperspirants can now be purchased for those who suffer from severe sweating. Products such as Drysol, Certain Dry® and Maxim can be purchased over the counter and are very effective at dealing with such challenges.

**Keep fresh**
During bathroom breaks, wash your hands with lukewarm water. Blot your hands dry with a tissue and finish off with a light mist of a clear antiperspirant. Avoid: Cold or hot water, air dryers and sticky antiperspirants.

**Seek medical advice**
Individuals with Hyperhidrosis may seek the advice of a medical professional or dermatologist. Both can advise and prescribe suitable treatments, such as: Prescription strength antiperspirants and Botox.

## Challenge: Eye contact

Good eye contact is one of the most important factors of body language. Shifty eyes, or complete avoidance of contact can suggest dishonesty, rudeness or lack of confidence. If you find eye contact anxiety provoking and uncomfortable, the following techniques will certainly help.

### Use a mirror
Practice your eye contact by using your own-mirrored image as a guinea pig. When you see yourself in the mirror every day, make a point of looking directly into your own eyes.

### Fake it
Rather than look directly into the eyes, you can fake it by either directing your gaze at their eyebrows, forehead, or bridge of the nose. This is not a permanent solution by any means, but it will certainly ease you into the process.

### Avoid staring
In an attempt to forge eye contact, you may begin to stare. This can indicate aggression and make others feel uncomfortable. To avoid this extreme, lighten your gaze to keep it friendly. This can be achieved by allowing your eyes to go slightly out of focus.

### Use opportunities to break contact
If you have notes, you can temporarily break eye contact as you refer to these. Also, if there is a second recruitment officer present, this will give you another opportunity to break eye contact as you periodically direct your focus back and forth between the two.

# Challenge: Going blank

Even with all the preparation in the world, our mind can betray us and draw a blank at the most inopportune moment. If this happens, take a deep breath, remain composed and employ some of the following techniques:

**Refer to your resume**
Your resume provides an immediate memory jog in these instances, so refer to it as and when necessary. You may also want to jot down some key words or phrases inside a professional looking notebook beforehand.

**Wait a moment**
You don't have to always answer questions immediately. It is perfectly permissible to pause and collect your thoughts before proceeding with a response. In fact, taking the time to think through your response can make you appear deliberate and thoughtful. Answering without regard for your answer can make you look impulsive.

**Be honest**
If you don't have relative experience in a particular area, or simply don't know the answer, you need to be honest and say so. At this point, you could offer an alternative and or related answer.

**Stall**
If you feel you can get away with it, reflect the question back to allow yourself a little more thinking time.

**Stay composed**
Some recruiters will purposely throw in some curve ball questions to see how you react to pressure and think on your feet. In these cases, the interviewer is probably more interested in observing your reaction than they are about the answer you provide. So, stay calm and do your best to answer in a confident manner. In the worst case, simply be honest and admit you don't know the answer.

## Challenge: Involuntary facial motions

Unless there is a medical condition present, involuntary facial twitching and trembling are generally ensuing of overly stressed muscles, such as forced smiling. These distressing symptoms are especially pronounced during an interview when you feel compelled to smile, or are attempting to conceal your nerves. To gain relief from these symptoms, you simply need to control how and when you smile.

Maintaining a constant grin is not only unnecessary and uncomfortable, it will also look insincere. Gentle and understated smiles are more than appropriate for prolonged periods, and full-toothed smiles should be reserved for introductions and the occasional injection during conversation.

Next time you feel your facial muscles begin to tense, try relaxing your smile and see what a difference it makes.

## Challenge: Vocal paralysis

Under severe pressure, your voice may become partially paralysed. The physical symptoms of this may include stuttering, a weak and shaky vocal tone, or an unusually high pitch. These symptoms can be managed by adopting the following techniques:

- Speak in shorter phrases
- Slow your pace
- Control your breathing by using steady in-out breaths
- Maintain an upright posture
- Ignore the symptoms until they naturally relieve themselves
- Seek the assistance of a vocal coach

# Challenge: Fidgeting

Fidgeting, tapping and excessive gesturing with give the appearance of uncertainty, nervousness and unpreparedness. To effectively manage these movements, use the techniques outlined below.

### Identify
If you are unsure of any habits you may have, ask a friend, partner or co-worker for their views. Alternatively, record yourself in a short mock interview and examine the footage. Mark down any ineffective mannerisms you can identify (playing with your pen, drumming your fingers, touching your face or hair, clearing your throat, or rubbing your nose) and then begin the process of consciously eliminating each of them.

### Beware of props
Props can easily exaggerate any fidgeting, so if you have a pen, résumé or bag with you, avoid fiddling with them. Be equally mindful of jewellery, such as twirling earrings or a finger ring.

### Mind your hands
If the movements you employ are subtle, it is perfectly okay to gesture your arms and hands to endorse your words. Subtle means, keeping the movements below shoulder height and above the waist. If you find your movements become excessive or distracting, simply intertwine your fingers and rest your hands on the table or clasped loosely in your lap.

## Challenge: Perceived arrogance

Sometimes, a high level of confidence may be misconstrued as arrogance. If you feel you are sometimes wrongly labelled as arrogant, the following guidelines will help you maintain your confidence, while avoiding this assumption.

**Be open**
We all have weaknesses; to say otherwise will certainly make you appear arrogant. Be clear about what you do and don't know, and be prepared to listen and learn from others.

**Be humble**
Act with humility when you are recognised for a job well done. Acknowledge the effort of others by sharing and giving praise where appropriate, and be accountable when errors transpire.

**Be approachable**
To make yourself appear more approachable, use open and inviting body language, and adopt a warm, friendly expression. Inject some personality into your conversations, make good use of eye contact and remember to use people's names.

**Be considerate**
Genuinely acknowledge and compliment the hard work and efforts of others. Listen to and respect others opinions, and avoid interrupting when others are speaking.

## Challenge: Being alienated

When there are a lot of different personalities in a group and the emotions are high, it can become difficult to get involved. This is especially true during a large group discussion. In these instances, you should employ some of the following strategies for getting your voice heard.

**Raise your hand**
As simple as it seems, raising your hand will demand the attention of the group and let them know that you have something to say.

**Be assertive**
If raising your hand reaps no results, you will have to be more assertive. Wait for a momentary pause in the conversation, and simple say, "excuse me" before proceeding. This may feel uncomfortable for some of you, but it is imperative that you contribute. If done calmly and respectfully, the assessors will be impressed by your effort.

## Challenge: Being ridiculed

If your idea is ridiculed, resist the temptation to retaliate. Instead, remain cordial and respectful in your response. This graceful reaction will be duly noted and respected by the assessors.

## Challenge: Handling disagreements

If you disagree with an approach being taken by the group or an idea, which has been brought forth, it is perfectly reasonable to say so as long as you are constructive and positive in doing so.

Consider the following statements:

**Negative**:
"That wouldn't work. I think we should..."

**Constructive**:
"I see your point, Mark, but there are a number of issues that may arise with that approach. How about we consider..."

The former example attacks and ridicules the idea, while the latter demonstrates a positive acknowledgement before a new idea is introduced.

In the instance that your new idea is rejected, remain polite and seek input from the group. If you are clearly outnumbered, gracefully accept the decision and move on.

# Challenge: Feeling uncertain

You don't always have to give an opinion when you speak. Supporting what someone else has said, asking a legitimate question, or commenting on an emerging theme are equally good ways to make your presence known without appearing as if you like the sound of your own voice.

**Points to Consider**
In most cases, the outcome of each task or topic is largely irrelevant. Assessors are more concerned with how well you perform in a team environment, how you communicate your ideas and interact with others, and what role you typically assume.

Thus, no matter how you feel, you should approach every task with a can do attitude and every topic in a calm and conversational tone.

> Find out what you like doing best and get someone to pay you for doing it

— *Katharine Whitehorn*

# MANAGE YOUR
## NERVES

# Manage
## YOUR NERVES

Nervous feelings before an interview are quite legitimate and most people can relate to feeling tense or fearful on the run up to such an event. In fact, a little interview anxiety can make you more alert and really enhance your performance, so you would never want to completely eliminate interview anxiety. However, when that anxiety becomes strong enough to negatively affect your clarity of thought and dialogue, some anxiety management techniques must be introduced.

# Prepartion
## AND PREVENTION

### Interview preparation

Anxiety can be the result of poor preparation. If you anticipate potential questions, prepare appropriate answers, research the airline and understand the requirements of the job, you will be better mentally prepared. If your mind is prepared, you will naturally feel calmer and more confident in yourself, and your ability to handle the interview.

### Remediation

Hypnotherapy, Cognitive Behavioural Therapy (CBT) and Neuro Linguistic Programming (NLP) sessions are very effective at dealing with deep-rooted anxiety issues.

### Medication

If you find your anxiety levels quite literally overwhelm you at interviews, you may be considering medication. While this is a method I don't personally advocate due to long-term side effects, there are over the counter supplements, such as Kalms, St John's Wort, and Bachs Rescue Remedy, which can really help take the edge off anxiety. Otherwise, your medical practitioner may prescribe stronger prescription medications such as Xanex or Beta Blockers.

# Manage your mindset

Limiting beliefs are erroneous assumptions you hold about your own capabilities. They lurk in your subconscious mind and lead to self-sabotaging behaviours, which prevent you from achieving your desired goals. These beliefs are mostly acquired subconsciously through outside influences and, once accepted and imprinted into your subconscious mind, will dictate how well you perform, interact and grow.

To move forward, these limiting beliefs must be identified and challenged, and then replaced with more empowering beliefs.

## Step 1: Identify

Clearly it would be impossible to challenge or change a belief that you are unaware of, so the first step to transformation involves identification.

Some limiting beliefs are obvious and can be easily identified by their all or nothing words, such as 'always' 'never', 'can't' or 'impossible'. For instance:

- My confidence always lets me down
- There's too much competition. I can't possibly compete
- The interviews are impossible
- I never say the right thing
- I always fail

Some beliefs, however, are so deeply ingrained within your subconscious that you may not even be aware of their existence. To expose these, you can use a brainstorming session.

Brainstorming is a simple, yet powerful, technique that produces raw material from the subconscious mind. To begin, simply sit down with a pad and pen, and start writing down everything that comes to mind about the interview.

If you struggle for a place to begin, you could use the opening line "I want to pass the cabin crew interview but..." then proceed to fill in the page until you run out of buts.

Asking relevant questions may also help, for instance:

- What meanings could I have created based on my past disappointments?
- What pessimistic thoughts reoccur every time I think about the interview?
- What unnecessary assumptions do I make about the interview?
- How might my standards be affecting my ability to relax?
- Am I holding onto any stereotypical beliefs that are holding me back?

## Step 2: Challenge

Now that you have identified your limiting beliefs, the next step is to challenge them. By challenging your old beliefs, you create doubt. This doubt is all you need to be able to slot a new empowering belief in its place. Strong beliefs are not always easy to destroy. These can, however, be weakened when they are challenged.

**Challenge the beliefs directly**
The first way to break down a limiting belief is to question its validity. Challenge yourself to find evidence against it, and build a case that proves the assumption wrong. You could ask yourself questions, such as: How do I know this? Is it impossible or just hard? Is there another way I could look at this? Could there be another truth here?

### Question the source
Do you know where your assumptions came from in the first place? Did you choose these beliefs or are they by-products of someone else's belief systems? Sometimes, realising a belief is not yours is enough to destroy it.

### Challenge their usefulness
During your life, you have picked up beliefs that have not served you or were only valid for a certain period, but you have held onto them ever since. Ask yourself: Does this belief still serve a useful purpose? Does it help me move closer to my goals? Does this belief help or hurt me? If this belief limits me, how can I quickly get rid of it?

### Weigh the consequences
The avoidance of pain is a great motivator, so realising the negative consequences of your beliefs may provide the motivation you need to destroy it. Ask yourself: What has this belief cost me in the past? If I don't change this belief now, what will the consequences be in the future?

## Step 3: Replace

In this final step, you will identify and install alternative empowering beliefs. To do this, you simply need to reinforce each new belief with sufficient evidence to support it. Ask yourself: What have I done in my past that could contribute as evidence? What activities and actions could I take now that would strengthen this belief?

Keep a journal and continue creating evidence towards it. The more ingrained you can make the belief, the more evidence it will begin to identify for itself, and the deeper rooted the belief will become.

This step isn't an overnight process. It does take time to imprint the belief deeply enough into your subconscious that it will stick long term and overpower the old limiting belief but, with repetition and reinforcement, positive changes will begin to happen in your life.

# Use your imagination

Since your brain knows no difference between real or imagined experiences, it is possible to use mental rehearsal and visualisation techniques to manipulate your physiology and improve your interview performance.

Find a quiet space where you're unlikely to be disturbed for 10-15 minutes and use these basic guidelines:

Get into a comfortable position and allow your body to relax. Take a few deep breaths and, as you exhale, imagine all of the tension slowly leaving your body.

Now imagine it is the day of your interview and begin to visualise the entire day, scene by scene, in your subconscious. When running through the events in your mind, imagine feeling relaxed, yet energised as you converse effortlessly with other candidates and the recruiters. Observe how others warm to your friendly and confident nature. Imagine your composure as you intelligently answer the interviewer's questions.

Make each scene as vivid and real as you can. Bring it closer, make the colours richer, sense the atmosphere in the room, and introduce sounds and feelings. Really intensify the experience.

When you are pleased with the imagined performance, begin to introduce challenging scenarios for different characters you may encounter, questions you may be asked, and pressure you may be put under.

Using this rehearsal technique for just twenty minutes a day will train your brain to actually perform the new skills and behaviours.

Repetition is the key to success with this technique. The more you practice, the better you will get and the more confident you will feel.

# Anchor your state

Anchoring is an NLP (Neuro Linguistic Programming) term, which describes a process whereby certain psychological states, positive or negative, become associated with and can be triggered by a certain stimulus.

Using certain techniques, it is possible to anchor positive states so that you can readily access them on demand, or you can break the association of undesirable states using collapsing techniques.

## Create an anchor

### Step 1: Identify
To begin the process of creating an anchor, you first need to identify the desirable state. For instance: confidence, calmness, and assertiveness.

### Step 2: Locate a memory
Next you need to recall a particular time in your life when you have felt the desired state. The context is unimportant, but the experience must have been a powerful one.

### Step 3: Get into state
With an experience in mind, mentally put yourself back into that experience. Use all your senses to make the experience as vivid and intense as you can. What did you see? What could you hear? Where there any smells present? How did you look? How did you feel? Now really focus in and intensify those feelings.

### Step 4: Anchor the state
When the desired state has been captured and the feeling is about to hit its peak, it is time to anchor those feelings. This is done by firing off a unique combination of cues.

The cue combination can include one which is visual, one auditory, and one kinaesthetic. For example, pinching the skin above your knuckles, while visualising the colour blue, and saying the word 'YES' is a unique cue combination that would be appropriate.

### Step 5: Repeat
To really condition the anchor, repeat this procedure at least five times. The more repetitions, the stronger the anchor will be.

### Step 6: Test
Now that your anchor has been installed, you need to test its effectiveness. To do this, you simply need to fire off your unique cue combination that you set up in step 4.

For best results, break state for a few moments and think of something completely unrelated.

If the anchor has been a success, the desired state should be experienced within 10-15 seconds. If the feeling is not satisfactory, further reinforcement repetitions may be carried out, or the power of anchor stacking may be introduced.

## Collapse and anchor

### Step 1: Identify
Before you begin the process of collapsing an anchor, you first need to identify the problem state (e.g. panic, anger, anxiety) and decide an alternative desired state that you would like to create in its place (e.g. confidence, calmness, assertiveness).

### Step 2 : Create
Next you begin the process of creating anchors (See above). First you will create an anchor for the desirable state you want to capture and then you need to repeat the process for the undesirable state you want to collapse.

In creating the se two anchors, you want to create the desirable anchor according to the steps outlined previously, however, the undesirable state should be created with less intensity in order to give the positive state more power.

This can be done effectively by simply visualising the negative state in less context, using fewer senses, and only using one kinaesthetic cue (be sure this cue is different to the one selected for the positive anchor)

**Step 3: Repeat**
To really condition the anchors, repeat the procedure at least five times. The more repetitions, the stronger the anchor will be.

**Step 4: Test**
Now that your anchors have been installed, you need to test their effectiveness. To do this, you simply need to fire off your unique cue combinations.

For best results, break state for a few moments and think of something completely unrelated.

If the anchor has been a success, the state should be experienced within 10-15 seconds. If the feeling is not satisfactory, further reinforcement repetitions may be carried out, or the power of anchor stacking may be introduced.

**Step 5: Collapse**
Finally, you can begin the process of collapsing your problem anchor.

To do this, you simply fire both anchors at the same time. As you do this, your physiology will feel somewhat confused as it tries to achieve both states simultaneously. If the positive anchor has been created strong enough, the negative anchor will begin to clear. At this stage, you can let the negative anchor release, while you continue to fire and hold onto the positive state.

**Step 6: Test**
To test the success of the collapse, break state for a few moments and try to re-fire the negative anchor. The result should be neutral. If the state persists the procedure may be repeated, using the power of stacking positive anchors.

# Ask resourceful questions

When you ask questions of yourself, you prompt your mind to search your internal memory archive for reasons and/or evidence to support those questions. So, whether you ask an empowering question, such as: "How can I achieve this?' or "Why am I so lucky?" or a disempowering question, such as: "Why does this always happen to me?" or "Why can't I ever get this right?" your brain will work to bring forth answers.

Wouldn't you rather have your brain bring back answers that create happiness and success? Well, why don't you make yourself a commitment to only ask empowering questions of yourself from this point forward? It's simple to do, and will really enhance the quality of your life.

**Replace:**
"What's the point? I never pass anyway"
"I always get nervous in interviews"
"Why can't I be confident?"

**With**:
"What steps can I take that will increase my chances of success?"
"What can I do to manage my emotions?"
"How can I feel confident right now?"

## Create Compelling Reasons

There may be challenging periods that arise during your interview, which cause you to question your motives. If you have compelling reasons for wanting the job, your conviction will give you the driving force you need to carry you through these challenging moments.

So, ask yourself:
Why do I really want this job?
How will this job change my life?
How will I feel when I am successful?
What would I enjoy about the job?

## Affirm & Incant

Affirmations are short positive statements, which are repeated several times in order to impress on your subconscious mind. To perform an affirmation, you simply take your chosen statement, for example "I am confident and successful in everything I do", and repeat it several times in quick succession with all the conviction and passion you can muster.

An incantation is a supercharged affirmation, which also engages your physiology. This action of getting your body involved creates a much more powerful outcome.

Depending on how deeply ingrained your beliefs are, you may experience some strong resistance as your brain attempts to challenge the positive messages it is receiving. Thus, the effectiveness of both techniques relies on repetition, conviction and passion. The stronger your concentration, the deeper your faith and the more feeling you inject, the stronger the results will be and the faster changes will begin to occur.

# On-the-spot
## RELIEF

### Deep breathing

Deep breathing will steady your rapid heartbeat, strengthen your shallow breathing, provide your brain with vital oxygen and make you more alert. Be sure to expand your stomach as you breath in, and not your chest. This will allow a much deeper breath to be taken and will allow your lungs to fill with oxygen.

### Change your focus

What you focus on has a direct impact on how you feel and what you experience. Therefore, anxiety is heightened the more you focus your energy on it. To gain some instant relief, you could try changing your focus. Instead of thinking about how you are feeling, how you look or what you are saying, re-focus your attention on outside sources. If you are engaged in dialogue you could listen more intently. Wherever you can redirect your focus will be much better than focusing on your internal dialogue.

## Adjust your physiology

What you focus on has a direct impact on how you feel and what you experience. Therefore, anxiety is heightened the more you focus your energy on it. To gain some instant relief, you could try changing your focus. Instead of thinking about how you are feeling, how you look or what you are saying, re-focus your attention on outside sources. If you are engaged in dialogue you could listen more intently. Wherever you can redirect your focus will be much better than focusing on your internal dialogue.

" It is never too late to be
what you might have been.

*- George Eliot*

# BLOOPERS BLUNDERS
## AND FAUX PAS RECOVERY

# It happens
## TO THE BEST OF US

We've all experienced a blunder at some time or another, from the ill-fated slip of the tongue, to the embarrassing body blooper. You name it, it's happened to the best of us.

In everyday circumstances, bloopers, blunders and faux pas can be brushed off and, hopefully, forgotten. But what do you do and how can you recover if this happens during the all-important interview event? Do you laugh it off? Apologise? Pretend it never happened? Blame someone else? Make a sharp and speedy exit, or maybe a combination of the above?

Just in case the unexpected should happen to you on your big day, I have devised some stealth tactics and faux pas recovery tips. Hopefully you will never have to use them, but at least you'll have a strategy if you need one.

## Three effective approaches

Depending on the severity of the blunder, there are three ideal approaches you can take: The first is to simply ignore it and move into a smooth recovery. The second is to hold yourself accountable and apologise, and the third is to simply laugh it off.

So let's take a look at each of these strategies further.

# The smooth recovery

In many instances, you may choose to simply ignore it and move straight into a smooth recovery. This can be a great option if the blunder was mildly insignificant or barely noticeable. The risk with this strategy is that many will use it as a means to forge ahead and hopefully disguise their embarrassment. Unfortunately this urge to keep talking can make things worse if you are rattled or fixated on the blooper. Instead of making a smooth recovery, you may find yourself babbling.

After a blooper, it is natural to feel embarrassed, but it is important that you don't become fixated or concerned about the blunder or the recruiter. You'll stand a much better chance of recovery if you stop, take a breath, smile and continue on.

# The artful apology

For moments that cannot just be ignored or brushed aside, there is the artful apology. Apologising for a blunder or faux pas is a great way to demonstrate a sense of respect and character. Rather than trying to hide or make excuses, drawing attention to the mistake and then apologising will demonstrate that you are honest and not afraid to take responsibility. This is an admirable quality and should not be underestimated.

Most people are willing to forgive, and you'll be amazed at how disarming a simple apology can be. Moreover, once a genuine apology has been made, the case is closed and everyone can move on from it.

It is important to keep your apology simple, yet sincere. A statement such as "I do apologise, my nerves got away from me there" or "I'm sorry, that came out wrong. May I rephrase that answer?" is all that is required. Once the apology has been made, shift the attention away and continue as if nothing happened. Don't give in to the urge to offer a lengthy apology, and don't bring the incident up again.

## Be willing to laugh at yourself

When all else fails, having a laugh at your own expense may be the only way to disarm your audience and smooth over the faux pas. It will certainly lighten any awkwardness that has emerged in the atmosphere and most people appreciate someone who is willing to laugh at their own mistakes. If nothing else, it will show that are you aren't easily rattled and at least have a sense of humour. Not bad qualities I'm sure you'll agree.

## It's how you handle it that counts

Whatever blunder you encounter, remember that everyone makes mistakes, and it is how you handle the mistake that will be observed and remembered. So whether it is the unexpected burst of flatulence, the skirt caught in the panties or a flubbed answer, if you are able to keep your cool and make a smooth recovery, the recruiter will appreciate your ability to remain composed in a challenging situation.

BOOST YOUR
# CANDIDACY
PART 4

# Contents
## Of this Session

**11** Application guidance

**12** Resume guidance

**13** Produce polished photographs

**14** Power up your portfolio

> If you change the way you look at things, the things you look at change

*- Dr. Wayne Dyer*

# APPLICATION
## GUIDANCE

# Ulterior Motives

It is true to say that job applications are primarily used to collect data for the purpose of evaluating skills, qualifications, employment history and motives, however, what most individuals don't realise is that there is an ulterior motive.

From the airline's perspective, the form serves a number of other important purposes, namely: To evaluate the applicant's literacy, ability to follow instructions, penmanship and communication skills. Recruiters will be looking or any excuse to thin the pack, so a careless applicant, or one who doesn't follow instructions, will quickly disqualify themselves, and the recruiter will not take the time to decipher what is written on it.

Unlike resume's, which are unique to each individual, the standardised format of an application form allows selectors to quickly peruse and compare each form, and it is easy to see which candidates have made an effort and those who haven't.

Consider the following examples.

| I CURRENTLY WORK AS A FREELANCE HAIRDRESSER AND HAVE WORKED IN CLIENT FACING ROLES FOR MORE THAN 8 YEARS. I AM LOOKING FOR A CHANGE IN MY LIFE DIRECTION AND FEEL THAT A CAREER AS CABIN CREW WILL GIVE ME THIS. | I curently work as freelance hairdresser & have worked in client facing roles fore more than 8 years. I am looking for a change in my life direction and feel that ~~that~~ a career as cabin crew will give me this. |
|---|---|

The first example is tidy and creates a positive impression of the candidate. Meanwhile, the second example is messy, full of typos and barely legible. It is clear that the candidate jumped straight in without planning. Hardly a positive first impression.

To ensure this doesn't happen to your application form, take note of the following guidelines.

# Important

## GUIDELINES

### Before you begin

- Read through the form to familiarise yourself with the questions and any specific instructions
- Gather materials: Black pens, a pencil and eraser
- Gather the necessary information:
    - Personal details: Passport, contact information, vital statistics
    - Education and training information: Qualifications, dates, results
    - Employment History: Names, addresses, key dates
- Plan what you want to write in each section, taking note of the space available

## Completing the form

- Set aside sufficient time and minimise distractions
- Re-read the instructions as you work on each section
- Write clearly and neatly: Block capitals are tidy and easy to read
- Keep your text within the space provided (Practice on a blank sheet of paper if you are unsure of the space available)
- Answer every question and use 'Not Applicable' or 'N/A' where questions are not relevant to you
- Keep the tone positive and be mindful not to volunteer negative information
- Be concise and avoid continuations on separate sheets of paper. If unavoidable, remember to clearly state your name and detail which part of the application form it is linked to

## Finishing off

- If time permits, walk away for a few hours and return with a fresh pair of eyes
- Finish off with a quick proofread and make any necessary adjustments if there are typos, grammatical errors and inaccuracies
- If time permits, make a copy of the final form for future reference

## Mailing off the form

- Select an envelope that is large enough not to require any folding of the form
- Address the envelope correctly and apply the correct postage
- Send it off before the closing date

# Stretching
## THE TRUTH

If you are thinking about padding out your application form in order to increase your chances of being hired, you wouldn't be the first. Many candidates are tempted to stretch the truth either to gain a favourable advantage or as a means to cover undesirable facts.

Airlines are savvy to this idea and often verify the details you include within it. So, beware that exaggerations and untruths can come back to haunt you if you are quizzed about them at the interview, or later in employment. If you are caught, any future you may have had with the airline will be devastated.

What are the chances of your information being verified? 100%. This is an industry that places high importance on security, and an airline is not going to take any risks with providing airside passes to just anyone. Your references will be contacted and your background checked, so be safe and don't take any unnecessary risks. There are many things you can do to boost your candidacy and minimise imperfections, and it just isn't worth the risk.

# Minimise

## A FRAGMENTED WORK HISTORY

A fragmented work history will give the impression of a job hopper and will raise serious doubts about your commitment. Whether the assumption is true or not, it surely doesn't present a favourable impression,

Whatever the reason, whether you have held temporary agency contracts, have been struggling to find something that you can feel committed to, or have simply been trying to gain a more rounded skill-set, it is important to draw attention away from it so that you can avoid any negative and rash assumptions being made.

Here are some options:

### Eliminate

Where a position holds little or no relevance, was held only briefly, is dated, or was only held part time, you may be able to safely exclude it from your application. Beware that you should only do this if doing so will not create damaging gaps.

# Spring into summer

Instead of listing specific dates for summer jobs, you can simply state Summer 20xx to Spring 20xx.

# Consecutive combining

Where several similar consecutive jobs appear or were provided by the same agency, you can combine them into one chunk, for example:

2004–2006 Receptionist
Aztec Hotel & Spa, Bloomfields Leisure, Trina's Hair & Beauty Salon

2001–2003 Customer service manager
Multi-national business agency

# Fill gaps in employment

If you have gaps in your employment history, you may be asked to elaborate on these. Whatever your reasons: whether it was for maternity leave, study or a travel break, you need to observe caution about revealing too much about your personal circumstances. Revealing that you had taken maternity leave will highlight your parental status and could be used as a tool to discriminate against you.

If you were doing anything during the gaps, paid or unpaid, inserting them in place of the gap will add much needed bulk and minimise the appearance of the gaps.

For example:

Summer 2004–Spring 2005     Travelled around Europe
July 2001–November 2001     Study break

# Never admit TO BEING ~~FIRED~~

When it comes to lying, there is one exception to the rule and that is if you have a termination on your record. The recruiters will not care if the termination was unjust, unfair or has a good explanation, a termination is a big red flag and will mark the end of your interview so you need to do everything you can to avoid disclosing it.

In the first instance, you may choose to omit the information. Omitting details is not the same as telling an outright lie or making a false statement. When asked for reference details, simply choose another referee.

If you have just been fired from your most recent employment, they will not know unless you tell them. So you could mark your employment to present and leave it at that. If asked if they can call your employer for a reference, it would not raise any eyebrows if you respectfully decline due to your ongoing employment.

The third option is to take proactive measures to have the termination designation changed. If the termination occurred some time ago, it is more likely that the employer will be open to changing the designation if you accept responsibility and demonstrate a sincere regret for the situation. Simply advise them that the termination is damaging your chances of gaining employment and you would like the designation changed to something neutral, such as laid off or resigned.

If you would feel uncomfortable or unethical to omit such a detail and would prefer to take accountability for what happened, be sure to downplay the termination on your application form by simply stating 'will explain at interview'. You will have some damage control to contend with, so remember to accept the mistake, don't blame others and don't make any excuses. Stick to the facts, point out what went wrong and what you have learned from the experience.

Whichever route you take, there is a risk. Either you not be hired by admitting to the termination or you may not be hired because you did not disclose it and were caught out. The decision has to be yours.

# Age DISCRIMINATION

Unfortunately, age discrimination does occur within the airline industry, so you need to take proactive measures to you protect yourself if you are a mature candidate. Lengthy employment is often a clear indication of your age, as are graduation dates. In this instance, you may consider omitting dates and providing only a partial employment history. While this may only provide a temporary level of protection, at least you can buy yourself some time to demonstrate your suitability for the position before it comes to light.

# Communicate

## YOUR SUITABILITY

The most important aspect of your application form is that you must communicate your suitability for the position clearly by highlighting the skills and experience that are relevant and transferable. Using a selection of key words that are often used to describe the cabin crew position will achieve this.

For example, a salon receptionist may include the following:

- Delivered the highest level of customer service
- Ensured customer comfort
- Provided a friendly and professional service
- Assisted with enquiries and resolved complaints

These short action statements identify customer service experience and the ability to handle specific responsibilities that are required of cabin crew. It would be clear to any airline that this candidate has the necessary experience and is adequately qualified for the position.

# Use
## ACTION PHRASES

When describing your duties, three to five action phrases have a better impact than complete sentences or generic job descriptions. Consider the following examples:

**Complete sentence**
'As a call centre officer, I answer customer queries and complaints over the telephone'

**Action statement**
'Addressed customer queries and resolved complaints'

The former example has a passive tone and is unnecessarily wordy, whereas the latter example uses an active and punchy tone. Such statements will grab the attention of the reader much more readily than lengthy paragraphs.

# Leverage
## YOUR LEISURE INTERESTS

Recreational interests create depth and humanises your character. A targeted list, which focuses on relevant skills, will form an immediate and positive impression. Such interests also serve as excellent sources of additional skills and experiences, which can be advantageous if you lack relevant experience in a work environment.

Generalised list statements such as: 'reading, watching television, sport and socialising' should be avoided, as should unprofessional statements such as: 'I enjoy spending time with my mates, hitting the town and going out on the razz".

Take a look at the following example:

"I have been keen on netball for as long as I can remember and am an active member of my local netball club where I have been captain of the team for 3 years. I have an active interest in nature, and regularly get involved with and manage conservation assignments. To relax, I attend yoga and meditation classes, which help to keep me focused and relieve any build-up of stress.'

This statement gives an immediate impression of someone who is balanced and committed. Their interests highlight several admirable qualities such as team spirit and leadership, and it also details their methods of stress management. A recruitment office would form a positive impression of the candidate based on a statement such as this.

Be mindful about over-indulging in your leisure interests, as the recruiter may get the impression that your hobbies will take priority over your work.

# The power
## OF A PERSONAL STATEMENT

At the end of most application forms, you will be presented with some form of additional information box. This box may simply state 'Additional Information', or it could be more specific, such as: Please state your reason for applying and why you feel you are suited to the position of cabin crew?

Essentially, this is an opportunity to sell yourself and should never remain blank. Use it to provide a power statement that summarises your experience, highlights your key skills, and shares your motives all within a few short paragraphs.

Consider the following example:

'As you will note, I have eight years experience within the retail industry. Within which, I have built extensive customer relations, team working and supervisory experience, which has also greatly enhanced my communication and interpersonal skills.

With these skills and experiences, combined with my passion for the airline industry, my motivation to succeed, strong attention to detail, and unparalleled work ethic, I am confident that I will make a positive contribution to the airline and excel as a member of the Fly High cabin crew team.'

The above example is concise. It focuses on what the candidate can offer the airline, rather than what the airline can offer the candidate, and it showcases skills and experiences that are an asset for a cabin crew position.

## Highlight career progression

If you have remained with an employer for several years, but have progressed through the ranks, you can make your progression more obvious by listing each position as you would a new job.

## List your awards

Outstanding excellence will show commitment and talent, so if you have achieved any awards through your activities, be sure to list them. Make sure the achievements are recent though, as outdated awards may give the impression that you haven't achieved anything since.

## Get permission from referees

Always get permission from the person(s) you state as your referee(s) and give them a copy of your application form or resume to help them write a relevant reference that highlights your most important points.

**FOR OFFICE USE ONLY**
Reference:          Base:

# Fly High Airlines

Application for Cabin Crew Employment

All information supplied will be treated as confidential.
Subject to meeting the eligibility criteria, you will be invited to attend our next selection day.
Correct information will be a condition of employment.

Full Name (Mr / Mrs / Ms)   **JANE DOE**          Date Available   **29/01/11**

## Present Address
22 Any Street
Any TowN
ANY WHERE

Post Code  **AN2 6DG**   Country  **U.K**

## Permanent Address (If different)
N/A

Post Code  **N/A**   Country  **N/A**

Please give telephone numbers in the format: Country Code + City/Mobile Code + Phone Number

| | Present | Permanent |
|---|---|---|
| Telephone (Residence) | 44 1179 637264 | N/A |
| Telephone (Mobile) | 44 798 837472 | N/A |
| Email | Jane.doe@anymail.com | |

## Personal Information

| | | | |
|---|---|---|---|
| Passport Number: | 2048374638 | Expiry Date: | 09/2021 |
| Date of Birth: | 11/09/1979 | Gender: | female |
| Marital Status: | single | Nationality: | british |
| Height (cm) | 154 | Weight (kg) | 49 |
| Do you have tattoos or body piercings? | No | If yes, please specify | N/A |
| How would you rate your ability to swim? | AVERAGE ABILITY unaided | | |

## Education
Please continue on a separate sheet if necessary

| From | To | Name & Address of School/College | Subject(s) | Results |
|---|---|---|---|---|
| 09/99 | 07/01 | Any college - any where - an8 7kd | hairdressing | nvq 3 - distinction |
| 09/98 | 07/99 | Any college - any where - an8 7kd | hairdressing | nvq 2 - merit |
| 09/97 | 07/98 | Any college - any where - an8 7kd | hairdressing | nvq 1 - distinction |
| 09/91 | 07/96 | any school - any where - an8 375 | english / geography french / art / cdt maths / science / maths | 8 gcse's grade a-c |

| Present/Last Employer | | | | | |
|---|---|---|---|---|---|
| Employer: | Self employed | From: | 01/02/03 | To: | Present |
| Position: | Hairdresser | Salary: | 15,000 pa | | |
| Address: | n/a | Notice Required: | None | | |
| | | Reason for Leaving: | To pursue a career as cabin crew | | |
| Responsibilities: | Manage and maintain a customer base of over 100 clients<br>Consult and advise customers<br>Ensure customer satisfaction<br>Provide a friendly and professional service<br>Maintain up to date records and accounts | | | | |

### Previous Employment — Please continue on a separate sheet if necessary

| | | | | | |
|---|---|---|---|---|---|
| Employer: | Trina's hair salon | From: | 16/02/00 | To: | 01/02/03 |
| Address: | 159 Any city centre any town - an9 6dj | Responsibilities: | Supervised and trained a team of four junior-level stylists - Hired work experience students - Consulted and advised customers - Ensured customer comfort and satisfaction - Provided a friendly and professional service | | |
| Position | senior hair stylist | | | | |
| Reason for Leaving: | to pursue freelance opportunity | | | | |

| | | | | | |
|---|---|---|---|---|---|
| Employer: | Trina's hair salon | From: | 05/04/98 | To: | 16/08/00 |
| Address: | 159 Any city centre any town - an9 6dj | Responsibilities: | Consulted and advised customers - Ensured customer comfort and satisfaction - Provided a friendly and professional service | | |
| Position | junior hair stylist | | | | |
| Reason for Leaving: | to pursue promotion opportunity | | | | |

| | | | | | |
|---|---|---|---|---|---|
| Employer: | MACEY's hair salon | From: | 24/07/97 | To: | 05/04/98 |
| Address: | 378 Any city centre any town - an5 6sj | Responsibilities: | Delivered the highest level of customer service - Ensured customer comfort - Provided a friendly and professional service - Assisted with enquiries and resolved complaints | | |
| Position | receptionist | | | | |
| Reason for Leaving: | to pursue promotion opportunity | | | | |

**Please explain any gaps in unemployment**

upon leaving school in 1996, i spent a year travelling before moving into employment

**Please list any voluntary work**

For the last three years, i have volunteered at the samaritans homeless shelter during the christmas period, where i help cook and serve beverages

Additional Training
Give details of any first aid and/or nursing qualifications

british red cross - basic first aid training - 09/2006

Give details of languages spoken and abilities

English - native language
french - read, write and speak fluently
spanish - basic conversational ability

Give details of any other training

i have attended, and passed, short courses in leadership and communication

---

Hobbies/Outside Interests

I have been keen on netball for as long as I can remember and am an active member of my local netball club where I have been captain of the team for 3 years. I have an active interest in nature, and regularly get involved with and manage conservation assignments. To relax, I attend yoga and meditation classes, which help to keep me focused and relieve any build-up of stress

---

Use the following space to provide any further information that you feel will benefit your application

As you will note, I have eight years experience within the retail industry. Within which, I have built extensive customer relations, team working and supervisory experience, which has also greatly enhanced my communication and interpersonal skills.

With these skills and experiences, combined with my passion for the airline industry, my motivation to succeed, strong attention to detail, and unparalleled work ethic, I am confident that I will make a positive contribution to the airline and excel as a member of the Fly High cabin crew team.

---

Declaration
Have you ever been convicted of a criminal offence which, at the date of application, is not a spent conviction as defined in the Rehabilitation of Offenders Act 1974?     Yes/**No**
If yes, then such convictions must be disclosed below.

n/a

Have you ever been refused entry, or deported from a foreign country?     Yes/**No**
If yes, please provide further details.

n/a

---

The details provided on this application are correct to my knowledge and belief. I understand that my application may be rejected or that I may be dismissed for withholding relevant information or giving false information. I am aware that my employment with Fly High Airlines will be subject to satisfactory references, medical form and criminal record checks.

Signature                                         Date           05/01/2011

Don't tell me the sky's the limit when there are footprints on the moon

*- Paul Brandt*

# RESUME
## GUIDANCE

# Influence
## THE DIRECTION OF THE INTERVIEW

Because the recruiters will have no information about you beyond this document, it will be a major influence in the nature and direction of the interview. This allows an element of predictability and makes it a very powerful document indeed.

With such a valuable tool at your disposal, it is important that it represents the best you have to offer. If your resume is strong, it will focus the recruiter's questioning on information that presents your image strongly. The following guidelines will help you achieve this.

# Appearance

## Colour
Use colour sparingly. Black text, with a consistent injection of colour for the headings will make your resume more pleasing to the human eye. Colour paper should be avoided as scanning or photocopying will be problematic.

## Length
For this type of position, one or two pages is ideal. However, don't be constrained by this advice if doing so will mean that you have to squeeze your data in and use a tiny 8 point font, If you do find your resume going beyond this quota, be sure that it isn't being filled with unnecessary, unfocused or excessive detail.

## Single or double sided?
Double sided prints are harder to photocopy and risk show through. Stick to single sided prints for a cleaner look.

## Staples
Never staple your sheets together. Staples are inconvenient for the employer if they need to photocopy or scan your resume, plus the reviewer may want to view the pages side by side. A traditional paper clip is acceptable.

## Identification
Be sure all of the pages include your name and page numbers so they can be easily reconnected should they become separated.

# A computer
## COULD BE DECIDING YOUR FATE

To facilitate more efficient processing of resumes, some larger airlines use a computerised tracking system. This system uses OCR (Optical Character Recognition) technology, whereby incoming resumes are scanned as a graphic image, converted back into text, read and added to the database.

With this in mind, it is important to write and format your resume in such a way that it can be successfully processed by these sophisticated systems. In this instance, the following guidelines apply:

The system scans your resume for keywords that indicate your skills, qualifications and experience. Following the scan, a score will be awarded based on the number of 'hits'. From this score, the system will either generate a letter of invitation, or a letter of rejection.

To ensure a high score, and an invitation letter, it is essential that you inject as many keywords as possible throughout your resume. The following highlighted keywords are the most widely scanned for:

- Good communication and interpersonal skills
- A confident and friendly personality
- Extensive customer service experience
- Confidence in dealing with a range of people
- The ability to work effectively in a team
- Ability to handle difficult customers firmly and politely
- Ability to stay calm, composed and focused under pressure
- The ability to be tactful and diplomatic, but also assertive when necessary

# Action
## VERBS

Action verbs express action. They are positive, powerful and directive, and should be used abundantly throughout your résumé.

Notice how using direct action verbs make the sentence powerful:

"As a hairdresser, I <u>consulted</u> with clients and <u>provided</u> advice"

The following page contains an extensive list of action verbs. Use them abundantly throughout your resume and application form.
There are three basic resume formats:

# Action verbs

| | | | |
|---|---|---|---|
| Achieved | Corresponded | Informed | Promoted |
| Addressed | Counselled | Initiated | Publicised |
| Advocated | Created | Inspected | Recommended |
| Allocated | Critiqued | Instituted | Recruited |
| Analysed | Customised | Integrated | Reduced |
| Anticipated | Delegated | Interpreted | Referred |
| Appraised | Demonstrated | Interviewed | Repaired |
| Approved | Designed | Introduced | Reported |
| Arbitrated | Developed | Invented | Represented |
| Arranged | Directed | Investigated | Researched |
| Assembled | Enlisted | Lectured | Resolved |
| Assessed | Established | Led | Review |
| Attained | Evaluated | Listened | Reviewed |
| Authored | Examined | Litigated | Revitalised |
| Balanced | Executed | Maintained | Scheduled |
| Budgeted | Expedited | Marketed | Shaped |
| Built | Explained | Mediated | Solved |
| Calculated | Expressed | Moderated | Spearheaded |
| Catalogued | Fabricated | Motivated | Spoke |
| Clarified | Facilitated | Negotiated | Strengthened |
| Classified | Forecasted | Operated | Suggested |
| Coached | Formulated | Organised | Summarised |
| Collaborated | Founded | Originated | Supervised |
| Collected | Generated | Overhauled | Systematised |
| Communicated | Guided | Oversaw | Taught |
| Compiled | Handled | Participated | Trained |
| Conceptualised | Identified | Performed | Translated |
| Consolidated | Illustrated | Persuaded | Upgrades |
| Consulted | Implemented | Pioneered | Wrote |
| Contracted | Improved | Planned | |
| Conveyed | Incorporated | Presented | |
| Convinced | Increased | Produced | |
| Coordinated | Influenced | Projected | |

# Format

## Chronological:

The chronological resume highlights the dates, places of employment and job titles, and is most effective for candidates who have a strong, solid work history. It is less effective for those who want to disguise gaps in employment or frequent job changes.

## Functional:

A functional resume focuses on skills and experience, rather than work history. Its ability to accentuate your transferable skills and detract attention from your career history makes it better suited to those who want to downplay an extreme career change or a chequered employment history. This style is less useful if you have limited work experience, as there will be little to highlight.

## Combination:

The combination resume, as the name implies, is a combination of the chronological and functional formats. It highlights both your work history and your transferable skills, and is most effective when you have a great deal of transferable skills and a solid work history.

For the purpose of a cabin crew position, I have listed possible resume sections below, in their suggested order:

# Outline

## Applicant information

At the beginning of the résumé, include your name, your home mailing address, your telephone number(s), and your e-mail address. If you have both temporary and permanent addresses, include them both.

## Objective statement (Optional)

An objective is a short statement, which defines your career goals. It gives your resume focus and shows that you have given consideration to your career direction.

Examples:

Seeking to utilise extensive customer service experience and exceptional communicative ability within a cabin crew role.

Seeking to pursue a cabin crew position with an airline that rewards commitment and hard work, and offers opportunities to progress.

Tip: If you include an objective, focus your attention on what you can do for the employer, not what the employer can do for you.

# Key skills (Optional)

The key skills section provides a fantastic opportunity for you to quickly express your suitability for the role and show what transferable skills your will bring to the position. Additionally, it will bulk out your resume with the keywords needed for OCR scanning technology.

Key skills to consider are:

- Communication Skills
- Interpersonal Ability
- Customer Focus
- Team Player
- Problem Solver
- Leadership

# Employment history

Your employment history should be displayed in reverse chronological order (that is starting with your most recent position and working backwards). This should include: the name of the organisation, the position held, the period of employment, the duties performed and results achieved.

The period of employment should include both the start and end dates, and can consist of only the month and year.

When describing your duties use action phrases, rather than compete sentences or generic job descriptions, and list any accomplishments that back up any key skill statements that you have made. For example, if you have stated 'extensive leadership experience' you can use a short action statement such as: "Supervised and trained a team of four junior-level stylists".

If some entries are more relevant to the cabin crew position, emphasise these and provide only summaries for those of less significance..

## Other relevant experience (Optional)

Employment history is a broad term that can include relevant internships, summer or seasonal jobs, part time work, and voluntary placements. This is especially important if you have little paid experience.

## Education summary

Starting with the most recent and working backwards, include the schools/colleges/universities you have attended. Within each entry, include the year of completion ("In progress" or "expected" are acceptable, if necessary) and award(s) you achieved.

## Certifications (Optional)

If you have attended any formal certification courses, e.g., First aid, life saving, then list the details here noting the institution name, date and certification awarded.

## Activities & Interests (Optional)

Recreational interests reveal a great deal about your personality and create depth to your character. They also serve as excellent sources of additional skills and experiences, which can be advantageous if you lack certain skills and/or experience.

Generalised list statements such as: 'reading, watching television, sport and socialising' should be avoided, as should unprofessional statements such as: 'I enjoy spending time with my mates, hitting the town and going out on the razz".

Here is an example: 'I have been keen on netball for as long as I can remember and am an active member of my local netball club where I have been captain of the team for 3 years. I have an active interest in nature, and regularly get involved with and manage conservation assignments. To relax, I attend yoga and meditation classes, which help to keep me focused and relieve any build-up of stress.'

This statement gives an immediate impression of someone who is balanced and committed. Their interests highlight several admirable qualities such as team spirit and leadership, and it also details their methods of stress management. A recruitment office would form a positive impression of the candidate based on a statement such as this.

Be mindful about over-indulging in your leisure interests, as the recruiter may get the impression that your hobbies will take priority over your work.

# Languages (Optional)

If you have more than one language ability, indicate whether you speak, read, and/or write the language, and include the level to which you are proficient, such as: native, fluent, proficient or basic conversational ability.

# References (Optional)

Unless specifically requested, the inclusion of reference information is completely optional.

When listing your references, be sure to include: Name, title, professional relationship to you (e.g. Supervisor, manager and team leader) telephone number and mailing address.

If you decide not to include details, a simple statement such as "References are available on request" is sufficient.

# Jane Doe

Seeking to pursue a cabin crew position with an airline that rewards commitment and hard work, and offers opportunities to progress.

16 Any Road • Any Where
Any Town • AN8 9SE
United Kingdom

+44 (0)4587 875848
Jane.Doe@Anymail.com

## Key Skills

Communication Skills
Exhibits exceptional written and verbal communication skills, and is adept at communicating effectively with people at all levels, and in a manner appropriate to the audience.

Interpersonal Ability
Unsurpassed interpersonal skills with a proven ability to quickly develop and maintain relationships with customers and colleagues.

Customer Focus
Experienced at providing a high quality service to customers at all levels, and skilled at effectively dealing with and resolving complaints.

Team Spirited
Skilled team player who adapts quickly to different team dynamics and excels at building trusting relationships with colleagues at all levels.

## Employment History

Freelance Hairdresser — Feb '03 - Present

» Manage and maintain a customer base of over 100 clients
» Consult and advise customers
» Ensure customer satisfaction
» Provide a friendly and professional service
» Maintain up to date records and accounts

Trina's Hair Salon | Senior Stylist — Aug '00 – Feb '03

» Supervised and trained a team of four junior-level stylists
» Hired work experience students
» Consulted and advised customers
» Ensured customer comfort and satisfaction
» Provided a friendly and professional service

# Jane Doe

Continued from page 1...

My confident and friendly nature will enable me to fit in and complement your existing team

## Employment History

Trina's Hair Salon - Junior Stylist │ April '98 – Aug '00

» Consulted and advised customers
» Ensured customer comfort and satisfaction
» Provided a friendly and professional service

Macey's Hair Salon - Receptionist │ July '96 – April '98

» Delivered the highest level of customer service
» Ensured customer comfort
» Provided a friendly and professional service
» Assisted with enquiries and resolved complaints

## Education Summary

| | |
|---|---|
| Any College (2001) | NVQ 3 - Hairdressing |
| Any College (1999) | NVQ 2 - Hairdressing |
| Any College (1998) | NVQ 1 – Hairdressing |
| Any High School (1996) | 11 GCSE's (grade A–D) |

## Certifications

British Red Cross │ Basic First Aid – Sept '06

## Languages

Fluent in spoken and written Spanish
Basic conversational ability in French

## Activities & Interests

I have been keen on netball for as long as I can remember and am an active member of my local netball club where I have been captain of the team for 3 years. I have an active interest in nature, and regularly get involved with and manage conservation assignments. To relax, I attend yoga and meditation classes, which help to keep me focused and relieve any build-up of stress

16 Any Road • Any Where
Any Town • AN8 9SE
United Kingdom

+44 (0)4587 875848
Jane.Doe@Anymail.com

" You have brains in your head. You have feet in your shoes. You can steer yourself in any direction you CHOOSE!

*- Dr. Seuss*

# PRODUCE POLISHED
# PHOTOGRAPHS

# A tool
## FOR HIRING DECISIONS

The requisition of photographs is so much more than a simple vanity requirement, and I cannot emphasise their importance enough. Not only will they serve as a visual reminder for the recruiters to refer back to throughout the assessment process, but they are also used to make hiring decisions long after the interview is over. Airlines place a great deal of value on the photographs, and some will even have very strict requirements about their presentation. For this reason, it is important that you use the following guidelines to create the very best lasting impression.

## Strict requirements

Each airline will have its own specific requirements, and these will be advised when you apply. As a general rule, a head and shoulder shot, generally in the form of a 45 x 35 mm passport photograph, and a full-length shot can be expected.

Both are subject to varying specifications and it is vital that you observe those to the letter. I am not kidding. There are some airlines who will not accept your application if the photos do not meet the requirements stated.

## Formal vs Casual

Casual shots, while acceptable for some airlines, carry the risk of appearing sloppy, unprofessional, and inappropriate. As a result, they present a much higher risk of rejection. Business attire will give the appearance of professionalism, and are often the minimum acceptable standard if you want to be taken seriously.

## Set the scene

A solid backdrop will produce a clean and uncluttered appearance. If possible, use a contrasting colour to avoid blending into the surroundings. And do not under any circumstances use a bed sheet for the backdrop. I've seen it many times and it looks very messy and unprofessional.

# Grooming

Photographs tend to exaggerate complexion issues and flatten your features. Use cosmetics to enhance your cheeks, lips and eyes, and apply concealer to diminish spots and blemishes.

Contouring and highlight is a technique that can be used to create depth, balance your face shape, play down flaws, and emphasise assets. Contouring uses a dark shade and is used to recede areas, while highlighting uses a light shade and is used to protrude areas. Try it out and see what a difference it makes to your look.

If you suffer from redness, the camera will pick it up and emphasise it further, so apply some green corrective concealer underneath your foundation to conceal it. Use these with caution as they are very heavy duty and can make you look very pale if over applied.

It is important to control the shine, particularly around the t-zone area, as it will reflect strongly in photos. For minor shine issues, a powder foundation should do the trick. For more problematic skin, an oil absorbing moisturiser or oil balancing gel may be more suitable.

Use eye drops to make your eyes glisten and clear any redness. And for wide awake eyes, try directing your gaze slightly above the camera.

Be sure your hair is neat and well groomed, as frizzy hair or loose ends can be exaggerated in pictures.

For an instant chin tuck, have the photographer position the camera at or just above eye level for the most flattering facial shot.

# Summon a warm smile

A warm and sincere smile will complete the look, but creating a beautiful smile on demand is a learned skill, which needs to be practiced.

The fake smile, aptly named the 'Pan-Am Smile' because of the flight attendants of Pan-American Airlines, is simply a courtesy smile that will not translate well in your photos. A 'Duchenne Smile', on the other hand, will provide the most beautiful and sincere looking smile, and this is the smile we are looking to achieve.

Here are some tips that will assist you in generating your photo perfect smile.

### Produce a natural smile

The most beautiful smiles are the ones that are natural. If you are using a professional photographer, they will be skilled at drawing out your natural smile, but if you are using an unskilled family member, you will need to channel some of your inner happiness. This can be achieved by thinking of a genuine reason to smile, such as recalling a happy memory, looking at a silly picture, or remembering a good joke.

Pan-Am Smile

Duchenne Smile

Copyright Paul Ekman 2003, "Emotions Revealed," Owl Books, 2007

**Fake it till you make it**
When it is simply impossible to summons a genuine smile, you will need to fake it. Here are some guidelines that will help.

**Time it right:**
The secret to producing a relaxed and natural smile is to time it so that you don't have to hold it for too long.  Try looking away from the camera, then just before the photograph is taken, face the camera and smile.

**Use your eyes:**
Smiling eyes are required to complete the look. To achieve this effect, imagine the camera is someone you really fancy. Raise your eyebrows and cheekbones a little, and slightly squint the corners of your eyes. Notice the amazing transformation this creates.

> "Never put off for tomorrow, what you can do today"

*- Thomas Jefferson*

# POWER UP YOUR
# PORTFOLIO

# Power up
## YOUR PORTFOLIO

### Boost your experience

Experience within a customer-facing role is vital, so if this aspect of your application is shallow or weak, you should certainly consider taking on some additional short-term volunteer or evening work to compensate and strengthen your candidacy. Taking on additional work will show initiative and demonstrate a willingness to work and improve.

### Take on volunteer work

Volunteering is beneficial to your application in so many ways. Firstly, it will demonstrate a compassionate and caring side to your personality. Secondly, it will enable you to gain experience and flesh out your skill-set. And third, it will show that you are not motivated by monetary gain.

As a side benefit, you will also gain additional referees who can vouch for you.

## Learn new skills

Taking the time to learn new skills will demonstrate your continued dedication to self-improvement and your effort in readying yourself for the position. So consider signing up for mini courses that will be relevant to the position, such as first aid, languages, assertiveness, communication, and leadership. Neither will take much time or money, but the value added to your resume will be substantial.

## Engage in extra-curricular activities

Extra-curricular activities can be a hidden gem when it comes to learning new skills and are often under-utilised. If you participate in team sports, it can demonstrate your ability to be a team player. If you coach little league, it will demonstrate your ability to be a leader and if you regularly participate in aerobic activities, it will show that you take pride in your health and fitness. So go out there and have some fun while boosting your candidacy all at the same time.

## Mind the gaps

If you are between work when you apply, this can create a damaging gap that will need some explaining or give the wrong impression about your motives. Rather than do nothing during this period of downtime, be proactive by taking on some volunteer work, learning a new skill or sign up for a short course at your local college.

### LIFTING THE LID ON THE
# GROUP INTERVIEW
## PART 5

# Contents
## Of this Session

**15** What to expect

**16** Hidden meanings behind the group tasks

**17** Sample tasks

> You become what you
> think about
>
> *- Earl Nightingale*

# WHAT TO EXPECT

# What to expect

The assessment process varies considerably in length and structure depending on a number of factors. These factors include: The volume of applicants, whether the sessions are held within the airline's premises or a hotel establishment, and whether the sessions are open or invitation only.

Open days typically attract a high volume of candidates and, as such, will often be split over a series of days. Invitation only days, on the other hand, are kept much smaller in number and may span only a few short hours with final interviews conducted on the same day.

In either case, you will be asked to partake is a number of activities. These activities are designed to reveal your personality, competencies and potential for working as cabin crew and are likely to include a series of individual assessments, practical tasks, group discussions and role-play scenarios.

Arrival at the event can seem overwhelming, especially when faced with hundreds of applicants in attendance. You will likely be met with an atmosphere that is friendly and buzzing with adrenaline, but has an eerie sense of tension, as each candidate is anxious to get through the process. This atmosphere generally tapers off as the sessions get underway.

# Complacency
## AND THE WAITING GAME

With large turnouts, the group will often be split into smaller, more manageable sizes, and assessed in rotation. This means that you will likely find yourself waiting around for long periods between sessions. Although you will not be in a formal assessment during these waiting periods, undercover officers are still assessing you and it is important to remain professional and alert.

Too many candidates allow themselves to relax during these periods, and it is when they relax too much that they become complacent. Just take a look around next time you are at an event and you will see candidates slouching in their seat and generally looking very bored. Don't allow this to happen to you. Move around and network with the other candidates. This will show that you are taking the event seriously and are a friendly sort. As a side benefit, this will make time pass quicker and make the day much more enjoyable. And don't worry about what other candidates will think, as oftentimes they will appreciate your efforts to lighten the atmosphere.

Session breaks are a welcome relief from the mental and emotional stress that the day can induce, but these are especially risky times for becoming complacent, as many candidates do not realise that they are still being watched and assessed.

# Just a number

Some airlines have negated to assigning candidates with numbers in place of using their names. This system of designation was introduced to streamline the process and to ensure that candidates are regularly shuffled. The idea behind the system is understandable and efficient, however, there is a disadvantage in that it leaves each candidate severely depersonalised. As such, you are no longer Kate, Alexander, Maria or (insert your name here), but instead you are number 284, 879 or 1029.

Such a system makes it all the more essential that you make an effort to stand out and be recognised.

# Avoid the traps
## DURING THE ICEBREAKER SESSION

The recruitment personnel will often start the day with a short introductory briefing and a breakdown of the intended days events. This session should last no more than 30 minutes or so, and allows for any remaining candidates to arrive before the event officially gets underway.

The icebreaker session may involve a short presentation about the airline followed by an open discussion session. During this time, candidates are encouraged to pose questions to the personnel about the airline and the position.

This session is an ideal opportunity to get noticed early, but it can also be a breaking point for those who are unprepared.

Many of the more confident candidates make the mistake of getting carried away with their line of questioning in an attempt to stand out. Unfortunately, asking too many questions at this stage will only demonstrate a general lack of respect for others, who also have questions, and is also more likely to be misconstrued as arrogant, rather than confident. One question really is sufficient.

In asking questions, there is also the added risk looking ill prepared if a question appears unnecessary or has already been answered within the airline literature. This will highlight your lack of research and does not create a favourable first impression.

If you do not have a valid and effective question, it is better to just listen and observe. There will be many more opportunities to get noticed.

# Stand out
## AS AN INDIVIDUAL

Once the groups have been arranged and applications submitted, the assessment typically gets underway with a short round of introductions.

As well as learning more about you and your background, these self-introductions are an opportunity for the recruiters to assess how well you cope when addressing a group of people and how articulately you are able to communicate your message while under pressure. In their assessment, they will be looking for good delivery and a certain amount of charisma.

To deliver a self-introduction that makes an impact, here are some guidelines for you to consider.

## Make it relevant

Use this opportunity to highlight your suitability for the job of cabin crew by sharing interesting facts about your present or most recent job, and your motives for making a career change.

## Be spontaneous

A self-presentation which is spontaneous, rather than rehearsed, will add life and sincerity to your speech. Sure you can prepare a rough draft and familiarise yourself with it, but don't try to learn it by heart, as there is a risk of appearing forced, dull and robotic.

## Inject personality

Show your passion and enthusiasm by injecting some emotion and personality into your presentation.

## Be concise

Unless advised otherwise, keep it relatively short and focused. Thirty to Sixty seconds should be sufficient.

## Rotate your focus

To give the impression of confidence and engage your audience, rotate your gaze and make eye contact with various members for three to five seconds each, then be sure to redirect your focus back to the recruiters to finish your presentation.

## Beware of how you sound

Varying your tone, pitch, volume and pace will eliminate the risk of appearing monotone and make it enjoyable for others to listen to. If you are nervous, you may be more inclined to rush. It will help if you make a deliberate attempt to slow your pace slightly.

## Consider this example

" Hi everyone. My name is Caitlyn and it's really nice to meet you all. I'm 27 years old and live in the bustling city of Bristol. I currently work as a freelance hair consultant, which is a job I really enjoy, but I have always wanted to be cabin crew, which is why I am here today. Outside of work, I enjoy horse riding and am captain of the local netball team"

# A process
## OF ELIMINATION

The primary objective during the early stages of the screening process is to filter and eliminate unsuitable candidates as quickly as possible. As such, you will experience periodic elimination sessions throughout the course of the day.

The initial eliminations will typically occur shortly after the first group session, but this is by no means absolute, as schedules are changed regularly and without notice. In any case, it is this first elimination that is the largest and it is likely that 80% or more will leave the process at this stage.

Most airlines will at least try to minimise the amount of stress caused by the eliminations, so they will usually be conducted on a group basis. As the day progresses, and the eliminations become fewer in number, individuals may be taken aside. It would be rare for any one applicant to be singled out or alienated in front of the group.

Naturally the elimination sessions are stressful, but if you make it through the first round, you can be sure that you have made a positive impression. Now as you go forward to the next round, take comfort in knowing that it will be much easier to stand out with fewer numbers in the group, so build on the impression that you have already created and give it all you've got. Use the adrenaline from your early success to carry you through.

> "Success is getting what you want. Happiness is wanting what you get"
>
> *- Dale Carnegie*

# HIDDEN MEANINGS
## BEHIND THE GROUP TASKS

# What recruiters
## ARE REALLY LOOKING FOR

This is the one question I am asked, time and time again. So many candidates overanalyse the process, but the answer is actually very simple. So simple in fact that most of you you will already know what I am going to say.

The recruiters are assessing six key competencies. These are:

- Communication skills
- Interpersonal ability
- Customer focus
- Team spirit
- Leadership
- Initiative

To determine these competencies, the assessors will be observing:

- ✓ Level of participation and interaction

- ✓ Behaviour towards the activities and your peers

- ✓ Communication and work style

- ✓ Ability to think on your feet and react to external pressure

- ✓ Ability to lead and willingness to follow

# Where confusion
## OFTEN OCCURS

Group tasks are designed so that assessors can view and assess these core competencies first hand, and how you behave during each task will be taken as a clear indication of how you may perform in reality. While it goes without saying that how you behave during an interview is not going to be an accurate representation when compared with a real life scenario, it is through your involvement and behaviour, that assessors can identify positive and negative attributes first hand and be able to make better elimination decisions.

Where most individuals often become confused is between the relevancy of the task and what is actually being observed. Because some of the tasks bear no obvious relevance to the cabin crew role, it is easy to overlook the underlying motives and get caught up in the practicalities of the task instead. And herein lies the trick: The outcome of the task itself is irrelevant.

# Focusing

## ON THE **WRONG!** ELEMENT

During this segment, most candidates are so intently focused on completing the task correctly and on time that they forget to think about their performance. In most cases, the outcome of the task is actually irrelevant. Assessors are more concerned with how well you perform under pressure and in a team environment, how you communicate your ideas, how you interact with others and what role you assume.

When you think back to the group tasks you have participated in, do you notice that they appear to have no right or wrong answer?

As an example, consider the following group topic:

## Topic:

The plane has gone down over the Atlantic Ocean. There are eight survivors, but the one surviving life raft only has a capacity for four people. As a **team**, identify four survivors from the following list who you would save and state your reasons why. Select a spokes-person to **present** your decision and explain why you came up with the answer.

- You (the flight attendant)
- An ex army general
- A pregnant lady
- An word class athlete
- The pope
- A surgeon
- A child
- A nurse

Clearly there is no right answer to this topic, as you wouldn't want to decide such a fate for four people. So what is the point of this task? Take another look at the topic and notice the words I have emphasised are 'team' and 'present'. These are the keys to this task. Assessors are looking to observe how you interact as part of a team, and whether you demonstrate initiative and leadership by volunteering to present the information back to the rest of the group.  Most candidates will focus on everything except for those two key points.

Let's take a look at another example: Singing.

Many candidates understand the concept of a discussion or role-play scenario, but just do not understand how singing bears any relevance. Again, this is very simple to comprehend if you read between the lines.

## Task:

Many passengers ignore safety demonstrations because they feel they have heard it all before. In an effort to increase safety, Fly High Airlines is considering an overhaul of its safety procedures. As a **team**, come up with a new safety demonstration, which will encourage passengers to pay attention to these important briefings.

The demonstration can include appropriate humour, and must be sung according to the melody given to you on the back of the card. The outcome should be no more than **five minutes** in length and **each individual must participate**.

# Seven
## HEAVENLY VIRTUES

### 1. Have fun

However silly or irrelevant the tasks may seem, your active involvement is essential. So, rather than concern yourself about external details, just relax and allow yourself to enjoy the process. This positive viewpoint will reflect well on your character, demonstrate enthusiasm, and make the experience a fun filled one for you.

### 2. Contribute

Contributing ideas and making suggestions is another great way to demonstrate your enthusiasm and team spirit. It will show that you are able to express yourself and are keen to get involved.

### 3. Volunteer

There are times when no candidate wants to put their neck on the line, so volunteering is a great way to demonstrate your enthusiasm and it will show that you are not afraid to take the initiative.

## 4 Summarise

Summarising the main points of a discussion is a great way to move past awkward moments of silence and sticking points. The breathing room summarising creates will typically stimulate further ideas and encourage participation. Not only will your peers be grateful for the momentary relief, your communication and leadership ability will also be highlighted.

## 5 Use names

Remembering people's names will demonstrate your ability to listen and pay attention to detail. Moreover, it will demonstrate a tremendous amount of respect for others and create a lasting impact.

## 6 Be positive

When you choose to exhibit a positive spirit, people will naturally be drawn towards your character. So, be enthusiastic about the exercises you are asked to undertake and be encouraging towards others.

## 7 Encourage

If any members of your team remain reserved, encourage their involvement by asking if they have an idea, suggestion or opinion. This shows empathy, consideration and team spirit.

# Seven
## DEADLY SINS

### 1. Over involvement

Getting involved and showing enthusiasm in a task is fantastic, but over involvement and incessant talking can leave others struggling to get involved and may transfer across to assessors as arrogance. Always provide others with an opportunity to provide their opinion.

### 2. Under involvement

For assessors to make an informed assessment, active involvement from each individual is essential. Those who are unable to get involved, for whatever reason, will surely be eliminated.

### 3. Disputing

Conflicting views are natural, however, a group assessment is neither the time or place to engage in a hostile dispute with other candidates.

## 4 Criticising

Even if your intentions are honourable and the feedback is constructive, criticising another candidates opinions, actions and ideas may be perceived as an attack. An assessment day is neither the time nor the place.

## 5 Being negative

Making negative remarks or exhibiting frustration over tasks, peers or previous employers , no matter how harmless it may seem, will raise serious concerns about your attitude and ethics.

## 6 Being bossy

There is nothing wrong with striving for excellence, however, being dominant and imposing your ideas on others is overbearing and intimidating. This always leads others to feel incompetent.

## 7 Neglecting to listen

Neglecting to listen to instructions leads to misinterpretations and displays a general lack of enthusiasm. Not listening or talking over others is ignorant and disrespectful.

# Active involvement
## IS ESSENTIAL . . .

I know it goes without saying, and I've covered this briefly above, but it bears repeating that it is only through your active involvement that recruiters are able to assess your suitability and identify your positive attributes. So however silly or irrelevant the tasks may seem, or how difficult it is to get your opinion across, your involvement is essential.

Rather than concern yourself about external details, just relax and allow yourself to enjoy the process. This positive viewpoint will reflect well on your character, demonstrate enthusiasm, and make the experience a fun filled one for you.

I understand that it can be difficult to get involved when you are in a group of individuals who have big personalities. They set off on a tangent, leaving you feeling like you are on the outside struggling to get in. While these conditions do pose a difficult challenge, it is absolutely essential that you do what you can to be included. Raise your hand if you need to, but whatever you do, don't remain on the outside.

If you suffer from nervousness, understand that it is okay to be nervous, even permissible, but allowing your nerves to keep you from getting involved is not. It is better to risk displaying your nerves than it is to remain silent. At least the recruiters will appreciate your effort. If your nerves are strong to the point that you become debilitated, turn back to part 3 for in-depth guidance, tips and tricks.

# . . . But
## DON'T OVERDO IT

Getting involved and showing enthusiasm in a task is fantastic, but over involvement and incessant talking can leave others struggling to get involved and may transfer across to assessors as arrogance.

If you do notice that other members of your team remain reserved or appear to be struggling to get involved, encourage their involvement by asking if they have an idea, suggestion or opinion. This is a clear indication of empathy, consideration and team spirit and it is these qualities that recruiters will be impressed by.

# Your scorecard

To make an effective evaluation, the recruiters will typically refer to a competency rating scale. This scale works on a points based system and the final result will reflect a candidate's suitability for the position.

| -1 | 0 | 1 | 2 | 3 |
|---|---|---|---|---|
| Unacceptable | Needs Improvement | Effective | Proficient | Outstanding |

| Score | Competency |
|---|---|
| 3 | Works effectively as a team member and builds strong relationships within it |
| 0 | Remains calm and confident, and responds logically and decisively in difficult situations |
| 3 | Understands other people's views and takes them into account |
| 2 | Contributes ideas and collaborates with the team |
| 0 | Takes a systematic approach to problem solving |
| 3 | Speaks with authority and confidence |
| 3 | Is thoughtful and tactful when dealing with people |
| -1 | Is conscientious of completing tasks on time |
| 3 | Actively supports and encourages others |
| -1 | Participates as an active and contributing member of the team |

" Go confidently in the direction of your dreams! Live the life you've imagined "

*- Henry David Thoreau*

# PRACTICAL TASKS

## Bridging the Gap

Duration: 30 Minutes

### Instructions

With the materials provided, design and construct a bridge which strong enough to support a roll of sticky tape.

### Materials

- 5 sheets of A4 paper
- A pair of scissors
- 1 Metre length of sticky tape
- 4 Drinking straws
- 1 Metre length of string
- 2 Elastic bands

## Let Me Entertain You

Duration: 40 Minutes

### Instructions

As you reach cruising altitude, you discover that the in flight entertainment system has failed.

To ensure the passengers are entertained for the duration of the four hour flight, design a game concept and present it to the rest of the group in a teaching style.

## Advertising Space

Duration: 40 Minutes

### Instructions

Fly High Airlines has secured a prime time radio spot and needs a new commercial campaign.

Using the team's collective knowledge of the airline, create a compelling commercial that will attract new customers.

The final broadcast must be no more than 45 seconds in length, and each team member must have an active role in the final presentation.

> **Points to Consider**
>
> This activity will highlight your knowledge of the airline, so be ready with plenty of input from your research.

## Designer Wear

Duration: 45 Minutes

### Instructions

Fly High Airlines is looking to update its image and needs new designs for its cabin crew uniform.

Consider the existing design and come up with a new or modified concept.

### Points to Consider

During this task, be mindful of what is considered appropriate to the culture.

Also, take inspiration from the current design as it provides valuable insight into what the airline considers to be appropriate.

" Just when the caterpillar thought the world was over, it became a butterfly "

*- Proverb*

# GROUP DISCUSSIONS

# Survivor

Duration: 45 Minutes

## Instructions

Your flight is scheduled to land in Los Angeles, however, due to mechanical difficulties the plane was forced to land on a remote island.

During landing, much of the equipment aboard was damaged, but 10 items have been recovered intact. Your task is to rank them in terms of their importance for your crew.

## Items

- A box of matches
- 15 feet of nylon rope
- 5 gallons of water
- Signal flares
- A self inflating life raft
- A magnetic compass
- First aid kit
- A fruit basket
- A tub of dry milk powder
- A shotgun

# Day Trip

Duration: 30 Minutes

## Instructions

You have been given the responsibility for arranging a day trip for 15 disabled children. Discuss where you would take the children, what activities you would have arranged and why.

## Options

- Theme park
- Museum
- White water rafting
- Trip on the Orient Express
- Water Park
- Safari
- Art gallery
- Scenic helicopter ride

## Points to Consider

In this instance, the children in question are disabled. So, certain activities will not be appropriate, while others may not sufficiently capture the children's interest. It is important to gain a balance between having fun and being safe.

> Too many of us are not living our dreams because we are living our fears
>
> *- Les Brown*

# ROLE PLAY
# SCENARIOS

# Role-play
## SCENARIOS

Role-play scenarios may be performed with other candidates as a pair or within a group, or they may be performed one on one with an assessor.

The scenarios will bear some relation to the demands of the job and are likely to include:

| | |
|---|---|
| Intoxicated passenger | Disorderly behaviour |
| Terrorist threat | Disruptive child |
| Toilet smoker | Abusive behaviour |
| Fearful passenger | Passenger complaint |

The assessors don't expect you to know the answer to every possible scenario they introduce. They simply want to see how you react in challenging situations. So, when taking part in any role play scenario, use the following guidelines:

- Be proactive and do your best to resolve the situation using your initiative
- Remain calm and composed
- Be direct and assertive
- Immerse yourself into the role
- Take each scenario seriously
- Devise a plan and follow it as much as possible

Here are some pointers to help you deal with some common scenarios:

# Complaint

In the case of a passenger complaint, it is important that you listen to their concern without interruption. Ask questions, where appropriate, to clarify their concerns and show empathy towards their situation. If the facts warrant it, apologise for the situation, explain what action you intend to take and thank them for bringing the matter to your attention.

# Fearful passenger

If a passenger is fearful of flying, be considerate of their feelings. Use a gentle and calm tone to talk them through the flight and reassure them of any sounds or sensations they may experience. Let the passenger know where you can be found and show them the call bell.

# Intoxicated passenger

Offer the passenger a cup of tea or coffee and don't provide any more alcoholic drinks. You could also encourage the passenger to eat some food. Remain calm towards the passenger, but be direct and assertive in your approach. If you feel it appropriate, inform your senior and seek assistance from other crewmembers.

# TAKE ON THE
# FINAL INTERVIEW
## PART 6

# Contents
## Of this Session

**18** What to expect

**19** Winning formula

**20** Guidelines for the most frequent questions

**21** Sample answers

**22** Ask the right questions

> The future belongs to those who believe in the beauty of their dreams

*- Eleanor Roosevelt*

# WHAT TO EXPECT

# What to expect

Congratulations if you have made it through to the final interview. Having assessed your involvement and performance during the group sessions, the recruiters have clearly observed qualities in your character that they admire, and would now like to explore your motives further. So revel in the success you have achieved to this point, and be ready to close out this process.

During the final interview, the recruiters will seek to explore your motives for applying to the airline and your desire for pursuing a career as cabin crew. Moreover, they will seek to gather information about your work history, character and work ethic to determine whether you will fit the job and airline.

To ease you into the interview process, and make you feel more relaxed, the recruiters will typically open the session with questions about you and your background. They will then seek to explore your motivation for applying to the airline and making a career change. Questions such as "Why do you want to work for us?" and "Why do you want to be cabin crew?" are common at this stage.

With the interview thoroughly under way, the recruiters will want to determine whether you possess the skills and experience necessary for the position. Here you can expect more probing situational and behavioural questions, such as "When have you handled a customer complaint?" and "Describe a time when you failed to communicate effectively".

Although there appears to be no typical duration for panel interviews, you can expect a baseline time of at least 20 minutes, to upwards of 1 hour or more. In either case, the duration has no bearing on your ultimate success; so do not overly concern yourself with this aspect. An interview lasting just 20 minutes doesn't indicate a failure, just as an interview in excess of 1 hour does not indicate success.

# Icebreaker
## OR DEAL-BREAKER

The interviewers will have several tricks up their sleeves to extract information during the course of the interview, but it is during the pre-interview 'ice breaking' session that you must be extra cautious.

During the first few moments of an interview it is only natural that most candidates will be feeing nervous, and it is under the rush of adrenaline that candidates are most likely to reveal too much information. It is also during these first few moments that candidates get caught off guard because they expect to be softly broken into the interview before the interrogation actually begins. Interviewers use this assumption to their advantage.

Personnel are trained to use trick questions, in the form of icebreakers, to get candidates to inadvertently volunteer sensitive and personal information about their circumstances and background. They will use friendly manipulation and small talk to lull candidates into a false sense of security. Under these conditions, they are able to extract information very easily from unsuspecting candidates.

So, whatever happens and however relaxed the interviewers attempt to make you feel, remember that you are being assessed and you need to keep your whit's about you.

# Meet the
## RECRUITMENT TEAM

Typically, there will be two or three official recruitment officers present during the final interview. These officers may be HR personnel, or they may be working senior crewmembers. Either way, you can be sure that they are experienced recruitment professionals.

To successfully interact with these recruitment personnel, it is important to understand their styles and be prepared to deal with them accordingly. Within a cabin crew interview setting, you will typically encounter two dominant styles of interviewer. I call these: The interrogation experts and the guardian angels.

## The interrogation expert

Interrogation experts believe that candidates will only show their true personalities while under intense pressure. As a result, they adopt a direct and intimidating style of questioning and will cross-examine every answer you provide. During this onslaught of questioning, they will be observing your ability to remain calm and think on your feet. So, approach their questions in a calm and confident manner and be direct and succinct in your response.

## The guardian angel

Guardian angels will attempt to relieve the pressure of the atmosphere by engaging in friendly conversation. While their relaxed and friendly style can be a welcome relief, unsuspecting candidates may become overly casual and reveal more than is appropriate. Caution is therefore advised to avoid being culled by these friendly tactics. You certainly don't to want to appear rigid, but you do need to be mindful of who you are talking to and remain professional.

# What assessors
## ARE REALLY LOOKING FOR

Recruiters understand that you will not be able to answer every question perfectly, and they also understand that you may not know the answer to each question that is asked. What they do expect and what they are invested in is how you respond to certain lines of questioning and how you conduct yourself. As such, their line of questioning will be designed to reveal your ability to:

- Listen actively
- Express yourself articulately, confidently and professionally
- Answer questions logically and concisely
- Remain calm under pressure

Some of the questions are designed specifically to throw you off guard, to see how you react to the pressure. With these sorts of questions, the interviewers are not necessarily looking for a perfect answer, but they are looking for a quick and well-prepared response.

They will also use several tactics to elicit a negative reaction or encourage you to reveal more than you should. This may be through the use of the silent treatment (as discussed in part 1), or through a line of questioning that is designed to keep you from knowing the correct answer. They will use trick questions, behavioural questions and even trick questions in the guise of a positive question, all in an attempt to rattle you and make you fall apart during the process.

Ultimately, it is important to remember that the recruiters are looking to hire positive people, so it is important to remain calm and composed throughout the interview and never show that you have been flustered.

# Seven
## HEAVENLY VIRTUES

### 1. Stay focused

If you fail to control your internal dialogue you will not only lose your composure, but you also risk misunderstanding the question. Remain completely focused on what the recruiter is saying and focus on giving the best possible answer. Concerns about how you look and the outcome should be postponed until after the interview.

### 2. Listen actively

Although you should never interrupt the recruiter, you shouldn't listen in total silence either. Instead, use verbal feedback cues to indicate that you are listening and that you understand. This will encourage the recruiter to continue. Some verbal feedback signals include: "I see", "Yes", "I understand", "Sure".

### 3. Inject personality

Injecting passion and personality into your answers will add life and sincerity. It will also keep the recruiters interested in what you are saying.

## 4 Be concise

If an answer is too long-winded, the recruiter will become complacent. Keeping your answers short and concise will retain their attention.

## 5 Vary your voice

Varying your tone, pitch, volume and pace will eliminate monotone and make it enjoyable for the recruiters to listen to. Slowing your pace slightly will also add clarity.

## 6 Be positive

A positive spirit will reflect well on your character and allow the recruiters to warm towards you. So, be enthusiastic about the interview and the job, and speak respectfully about your previous employers and positions.

## 7 Maintain eye contact

Regular, strong eye contact will give the impression of someone who is honest and confident. Where there is more than one recruitment officer, you should maintain eye contact with the person who asks you the question while occasionally engaging eye contact with the second recruiter.

# Seven
## DEADLY SINS

### 1. Controlling

Trying to lead or control the conversation will appear arrogant and disrespectful. Ask questions when appropriate opportunities arise, but allow the recruiter to do his or her job.

### 2. Interrupting

Interruptions are rude and disrespectful to the speaker. So, unless absolutely necessary, you should allow the recruiter to finish **speaking** before responding or asking for clarification.

### 3. Lying

If you lie, there will be a very good chance that you will be caught out when the recruiters probe into your answers with follow up questions. If this happens, you could end up looking rather silly and, worse still, any chance of being offered the job will be ruined.

## 4 Talking incessantly

It's easy to talk too much when nervous, however, it is important to remember that interviews are two-way exchanges. A moment of silence, while it might seem awkward to you, lets the recruiter know that you are done and allows them to move the interview along.

## 5 Being negative

Making negative remarks or exhibiting frustration over tasks, peers, other airlines or previous employers, no matter how harmless it may seem, will raise serious concerns about your attitude and ethics.

## 6 Overusing filler words

The useless and annoying verbal mannerisms "you know," "like," "in other words," "kind of," "ummm," and "anyways." should be avoided at all costs. Besides making you sound unprofessional, they also detract attention from your message.

## 7 Unprepared or unnecesary questions

To stand out as an informed and competent applicant, your questions should reflect that you have researched the airline and the position. Asking questions that have already been addressed within the airline's literature will make you appear unprepared and incompetent. Likewise, asking questions that are based on money and benefits will make you appear selfishly motivated and give a negative impression about your motives for the position and/or the airline.

# Avoid robotic
## FLAT AND BORING ANSWERS

In preparing for the final interview, it may make sense to memorise some of your answers. Unfortunately, trying to memorise an answer for every scenario will only work against you. Not only do you run the risk of sounding like a robot, with a boring and flat delivery, but you also risk forgetting your answers and appearing flustered as you try to recall the information.

Rather than memorising your answers, make a list of key points and try to remember those instead. Key points are much easier to remember than lengthy sentences and will allow you to create a genuine and spontaneous answer based around that point.

Another technique, that is highly effective and advantageous, is to prepare through actual practice. Whether that is through a role play with a friend or family member, the use of a camcorder or through attending mock interviews with other airlines, practice will allow you to feel much more confident and natural when you do the real thing.

## Demonstrate respect for the recruiter

It is important to be observant and sense when the interviewer has heard enough about a particular point. Many candidates go off on a tangent when they get into the swing of the interview, and neglect to notice that the interviewer wants to move on. To demonstrate your respect for the recruiter and his or her time, you could ask "Would you like me to elaborate on that further?" The interviewer will appreciate your effort.

## Eek, I don't know the answer

You are not expected to know the answer to every question you are asked. In fact, the interviewer may throw you a curve ball on purpose in order to test you reaction and observe how you respond under the pressure.

Bluffing your way through an answer, for the sake of not wanting to admit that you don't know the answer, will not reflect favourably on you. The interviewer will be much more forgiving if you are honest and admit your lack of knowledge on a particular point.

If you lack relative experience in a particular area, you may consider elaborating on a similar and alternative aspect, or you can take the opportunity to remind them of the skills that you do have and explain how you would tackle the situation if it arose. For instance: "I can't remember ever being in that situation, however, I did face something slightly similar that I could tell you about?".

# Run of the mill clichés wil not cut it

Answers such as "I'm a workaholic" or "I'm a perfectionist" or "I try too hard to please everyone" are tired old cliché's and are simply not going to cut it. While they may be true statements, recruiters are not naive and they certainly will not accept generic responses such as these.

Generic answers will only make you sound just like everyone else and will not do you any favours. You need to be more creative and, more importantly, you need to sound sincere.

# Stand out as an informed candidate

Taking the time to research an airline you want to work for will enable you to ask intelligent questions, as well as answer any that are posed. Your informed knowledge will give a positive impression about you and your motivation to work for the airline, thus giving you a competitive edge over less informed candidates.

If you know nothing about the airline other than the colour of the uniform, the salary and their best destinations, you certainly won't create a positive impression.

There is no need to know the whole history of the airline, but you should at least know some basic information, such as:

- What is their route network?
- Are there any future plans for expansion or growth?
- Where is their base airport located?
- Who are the airline's major competitors?
- What do you like about this particular airline?
- How long have they been operating?
- Has the airline won any awards? If so, which ones?

> "We are the hero of our own story"
>
> *- Mary McCarthy*

# WINNING
# FORMULA

# Answers
## AS EASY AS **A.B.C**

When preparing your answers to traditional questions, keep the A.B.C formula in mind.

### **A** Answer

Make your answer concise by answering the question directly

### **B** Back it up

Back up your answer with solid facts. This will add a lot of weight to any statements made.

### **C** Conclude

The conclusion allows you to expand on your skills and what you can offer the airline

Consider the following example:

# What is your best attribute?

**Answer:**
"As you will have observed during the group assessments, I am a very welcoming and social individual who interacts well with others, and readily adapts to new people and environments."

**Back it up:**
"In fact, my previous supervisor also picked up on these attributes and often asked me to carry out the client shampoo because she knew I would make the clients feel welcome and relaxed"

**Conclude:**
"I am confident that this aspect of my character will enable me to perform the job to the same high standard that exists currently within the airline"

# A.C.T
## ON NEGATIVE QUESTIONS

Negative questions can be better approached using the A.C.T formula.

### A  Attack

By attacking the question head on, not only do you avoid being alienated by the question, it also allows you to swiftly move on and add clarity to your response.

### C  Clarify

This is your opportunity to add any clarity and facts that may support or justify your answer.

### T  Turn

Now turn the focus away from the initial negative question to focus on the positive outcome of the experience.

Consider the following example:

# What is your greatest weakness?

**Attack:**
"I recognise that my leadership ability is a potential area of improvement"

**Clarify:**
"Which is why I am actively working on developing this area further through a part time training course at my local college"

**Turn:**
"Although I am still learning, I see constant improvement in my capabilities when being faced with leadership tasks and I am confident that I will continue to learn and grow with experience"

# Winning answers
## WITH THE **S.A.R.R** FORMULA

When preparing your examples to competency-based questions, the S.A.R.R formula can help you structure your response.

### **S** Situation
Briefly describe the challenge, problem, or task

### **A** Action
Describe what you did and how you did it

### **R** Result
Describe the outcome and how your actions affected the outcome or the people involved

### **R** Reflection
Elaborate on what you learned from the experience and whether you would do things differently in the future.

Consider the following example:

# When have you used your initiative to solve a problem?

**Situation:**
"I was in the staff room during my lunch break, and I could hear a lot of noise coming from inside the salon. I went to investigate and two, very bored, little girls confronted me. I could sense that their excitement was causing a disruption and inconvenience"

**Action:**
"I immediately took the initiative and attempted to occupy them by offering to plait their hair while they made bracelets from some hair beads. Their eyes sparkled with excitement and I was able to keep them occupied for the remainder of their visit"

**Result:**
"We had lots of fun and, while the calm was restored, the stylist was able to complete the clients' treatment"

**Reflection:**
"I felt really pleased that with just a little extra effort, I had made such a big difference"

# Probing with
## FOLLOW-UP QUESTIONS

Follow up questions are either used to verity the viability of your answer, or to tempt negative information into the open. So it is important to have examples ready to back up any statements made.

Prepare to be asked:

- What did you learn from the experience?
- What specifically did you say?
- How did you feel?
- Would you do anything differently?
- How did they react?
- What other options did you consider?
- Why did you decide to take the action that you did?
- You mentioned ... Tell me more about that.
- How did you retain your composure?
- Can you give me an example of that?
- Can you be more specific about...?

# The constant
## INTERRUPTION

In an attempt to throw you off, the recruiter may even interrupt your responses with supplementary probing questions.

Take a look at the following example.

## When have you disagreed with a colleague?

**Candidate**
"Working in a creative environment with other highly skilled professionals, it was natural that we had the occasional clash of ideas."

**Recruiter**
"Please can you elaborate further?"

**Candidate**
"We would sometimes have a clash of ideas based around our individual preference towards certain products, styles, magazines or equipment. Although, any disagreements we did have were relatively minor and insignificant."

**Recruiter**
"What would you consider minor and insignificant?"

**Candidate**
"Our debates were never confrontational, and they never interfered with our work in any way. In fact, some disagreements were quite educational."

**Recruiter**
"Educational?"

**Candidate**
"Yes, some very interesting views emerged from these debates which sometimes resulted in people, including myself, having a slight change in perspective."

**Recruiter**
"Can you tell me about a change you had in perspective following such a debate?"

...

---

It is important to answer the questions without demonstrating any frustration or resentment, Once you have answered the quesiton, smile and get straight back on point.

" To accomplish great things, we must not only act, but also dream; not only plan, but also believe

— *Anatole France*

# GUIDELINES FOR THE MOST FREQUENT QUESTIONS

# Tell me
## ABOUT YOURSELF

> This question is usually asked early as an ice breaker. There is no need to delve into your childhood leisure pursuits here, the recruiters simply want a paraphrased overview of what you do, why you are attending the interview and what you have to offer.

"As you can see from my résumé, I currently work as a freelance hair consultant, and have worked in client-facing roles for the past eight years. During this time, I have worked my way up from a receptionist to a senior hair stylist, while simultaneously studying for my NVQ levels 1, 2 and 3.

Now, this brings me to why I am here today, interviewing with you.

I have always wanted to become cabin crew and, during the course of my career, I have been gradually mastering the skills needed to perform its tasks. I'm confident that the customer care and teamwork skills I have developed throughout the course of my career, combined with my friendly and positive nature, will complement your existing team and enable me to deliver the standard of service that passengers have come to expect from Fly High Airlines.

I'd now like to discuss how I might continue my success by joining your team."

# Why do you want
## TO BECOME CABIN CREW?

An honest and passionate response to this question will surely set you apart. Think about it, why do you really want the job? Where did the desire come from? Was it a childhood dream, or was it sparked by another interest?

"As a child, I was fascinated by aircraft and always felt a buzz of excitement when planes flew overhead.

This is where my passion for flying initially began, but it wasn't until I carried out a career suitability test at college that I really started to consider cabin crew as a serious future prospect.

The test examined personal attributes, interests and skills, and the final result came back suggesting suitability for the occupation.

I done some further research into the job and instantly agreed. This job is tailored to my personality, skills and experience and is one I will feel committed to. Moreover, it is one I am confident that I will be good at."

# Why should
## WE HIRE YOU?

> This is the time to shine, so don't be modest. Consider the experience and character traits that are most relevant and transferable to the position and explain how you have demonstrated these in the past.

### Answer
"As you can see from my résumé, I have worked in client facing roles for the past eight years. So, I am certainly qualified to perform the diverse requirements of this role. Also, the fact that I have been promoted through the ranks is a clear testament to my abilities and the confidence my manager had in me.

### Back It Up
More significantly, my character is tailored to the role. As you will have observed during the group assessments, I am a very welcoming and social individual who interacts well with others. I readily adapt to new people and environments, I am hard working and think fast on my feet.

### Conclude
I am confident that these aspects of my personality and experience will enable me to perform the job to the same high standard that exists currently."

# Why do you
## WANT TO WORK FOR THIS AIRLINE?

> To make the greatest impact, begin with a personal story, but close with a demonstration of your knowledge and fit for the airline. This will make you stand out as an informed and enthusiastic individual who has something more to offer.

"My first passenger experience with Fly High Airlines was two years ago, on a flight from Dubai to Los Angeles. The service on board was so immaculate and welcoming, that I was instantly impressed. Following this experience I became a frequent flyer and, when I decided to apply for this position, I was in no doubt who I want to work for.

Once I started to research the airline further, I was pleased to discover that the airlines corporate culture holds true with my own values and beliefs. Specifically the open door policy and customer comfort initiatives. This discovery reinforced my desire further and confirmed my belief that I will indeed complement your existing team."

## What are
## YOUR BEST QUALITIES?

Don't be shy, give it all you got. But, be sure to back it up with examples.

**Answer**
"As you will have observed during the group assessments, I am a very welcoming and social individual who interacts well with others, and readily adapts to new people and environments."

**Back it up**
"In fact, my previous supervisor also picked up on these attributes and often asked me to carry out the shampoo because she knew I would make the clients feel welcome and relaxed"

**Conclude**
"I am confident that these aspects of my character will enable me to perform the job to the same high standard that exists currently within the airline"

# What is
## YOUR GREATEST WEAKNESS?

> The key to answering questions about weaknesses is to focus your response on those skills you are actively learning or planning to develop. This could be assertiveness or leadership. The point is, it is only a weakness because you haven't yet mastered it, and that is why you are working on developing those skills further.

**Attack:**
"I recognise that my leadership ability is a potential area of improvement"

**Clarify:**
"Which is why I am actively working on developing this area further through a part time training course at my local college"

**Turn:**
"Although I am still learning, I see constant improvement in my capabilities when being faced with leadership tasks and I am confident that I will continue to learn and grow with experience"

# What qualities
## ARE NECESSARY FOR CABIN CREW?

> The recruiters want to know that you understand what the role involves and what qualities are necessary to perform its tasks. Conclude this answer by acknowledging your skills in relation to the position.

"Cabin crew play a vital role in giving a good impression of the airline as a whole. This means crew members need to have good communication and customer care skills, as well as a friendly and welcoming demeanour.

Because of the importance of safety, it is also important that they have the strength of character to cope with difficult people and situations, in a calm and objective manner.

These are all attributes I possess, and are the primary reasons I would complement your existing team."

# Why did you LEAVE YOUR LAST JOB?

While you do need to be honest about your reasons for leaving past employment, you need to be diplomatic in your response. Being bored or not getting along with your boss are not ideal answers here.

- » No opportunities
  "While I enjoyed working for my previous employer, and appreciate the skills I developed while I was there, I felt I was not being challenged enough in the job. After working my way up through the company, there were no further opportunities for advancement."

- » Redundancy
  "I survived the first layoffs, but unfortunately this one got me."

- » Temporary position
  "The job was only a temporary position which I took to broaden my experience."

# What do you know
## ABOUT OUR AIRLINE?

> This is where your research will pay off handsomely. So, demonstrate your enthusiasm by sharing knowledge that will reveal the effort you have taken to learn more about the airline and its operations.

"Fly High Airlines began operating in 1980 with a single leased aircraft, serving just two destinations. The airline now serves 73 destinations in 48 countries worldwide and is rapidly expanding its route network, which is soon to include Bristol and Ohio.

As a testament to the airlines excellent standard of service, it has acquired over 250 international awards for customer service excellence, and is now one of the largest and popular airlines in the world."

# What do you dislike
## ABOUT YOUR CURRENT JOB?

> There will always be less than exciting aspects of a job, however, being critical about your job isn't going to create a positive impression. So, soften these aspects as much as possible and try to select neutral examples, such as paperwork, lack of job security or opportunities for growth.

"I honestly can't think of any major dislikes. I don't think I'd be able to really excel if I weren't truly interested in the work, or if I were merely motivated by its financial rewards. I guess my answer will have to come under the category or nuisances.

The biggest nuisance is the paperwork. I realise the importance of documentation, and I cooperatively fill out the forms, but I'm always looking for efficiencies in that area that will get me out in front of the client where I belong."

" When you walk with purpose, you collide with destiny

*- Bertice Berry*

# SAMPLE ANSWERS FOR BEHAVIOURAL QUESTIONS

# 1 When have you gone out of your way for a customer?

## Evaluation

Those candidates who demonstrate that they always put in extra effort to provide a better and more complete service will surely have an advantage.

Your answer should demonstrate that you always go the extra mile, and never deliver a merely acceptable standard.

## Sample Response 1

**Situation**:
I had a client call into the store who was looking for a very specific style of fabric. She had visited several stores in and around the area but hadn't been successful in her search.

I could see that she was exhausted, but also very determined. She spoke with such sorrow in her voice that I actually began to feel sorry for the poor lady because I didn't have the fabric to sell her.

**Action**:
Not wanting to be the bearer of more bad news, I decided to offer my assistance. I spent several hours ringing around wholesalers, distributors and manufacturers trying to track down this particular fabric, when finally I struck gold with a small manufacturing plant.

**Result**:
Because the fabric was a special order, there was a small handling charge, but the customer received the fabric within a few days and was sure it was worth the expense and wait.

## Sample Response 2

**Situation**:
I encountered a problem when one of my clients was unable to have a hair treatment carried out in her home because it was being renovated.

**Action**:
In an attempt to keep the client, I spoke to a contact I had within a local salon and was able to negotiate a small fee for use of the salon facilities.

**Result**:
This worked out really well because it was convenient for both myself and the client to travel to. Since then, I have negotiated similar deals with four other salons and have increased my customer base dramatically as a direct result.

## 2. Describe a time when your customer service could have been better?

### Evaluation

Providing excellent customer service is vital, so you should be very cautious when providing negative examples.

You could take a modest approach and explain that you always strive to do better, or you could be honest with humble example.

Alternatively, you could attempt to avoid providing an example by explaining how you maintain your standards, and then proceed with an example of a time when you have demonstrated this capability.

### Sample Response (Modest approach)

I take great pride in providing the best service I possibly can, but in doing so I increase my skills and can always see room for improvement.

### Sample Response (No experience)

I take great pride in providing the best service I possibly can, and I never let my standards slip. Even during times of high pressure, I make an effort to remain courteous and helpful. I can honestly say that I have never received any negative feedback.

# 3  When have you solved a customer problem?

## Evaluation

The recruiter wants to get an idea of how you apply your initiative and problem-solving skills to customer related issues. A good answer here will demonstrate that you always put in extra effort to provide good customer service and are not intimidated by difficult situations.

## Sample Response

**Situation:**
I remember a client who came to me to have her hair extensions replaced. She had worn sewn in extensions for several months and was experiencing some discomfort from the attachments.

**Action:**
As I examined her hair, I was shocked to discover how much damage had been caused. Her roots had become severely matted and the tightness from the installed tracks had created spots of baldness.

I took a moment to analyse the situation, work out a strategy and then I set to work.

I spent several hours meticulously untangling every hair and removing every extension piece, The more I removed, the more I could see the scale of the damage that had been caused. Sadly, the client's hair was in very bad shape after the removal and the spots of baldness were very evident. Needless to say, I had a very emotional customer.

I applied a very deep conditioning protein treatment to the customers remaining locks and gave it a good trim. I then finished up with some fine and strategically placed fusion hair extensions to conceal the bald patches and create some much needed volume.

**Result:**
Following the treatment, the client looked fantastic and her smile was restored. Her hair soon returned to its former glory and she became a regular client of mine.

# 4 When have you tended to an upset customer?

## Evaluation

The recruiter is trying to grasp your ability to cope with stressful situations. A good answer will suggest that you can think on your feet, and display a positive and patient attitude when challenging situations arise.

## Sample Response

**Situation**:
I recently experienced a situation with a client who was having relationship problems. She was becoming increasingly emotional and I could sense that she was feeling very depressed.

**Action**:
Although I felt compassion for her situation, I knew that it was important for me not to get overly involved. So, I gave her chance to talk while I listened, and I tried to show empathy while remaining neutral and professional in my response.

**Result**:
Just being able to talk to someone who listened seemed to make her feel better. As she continued to speak, she appeared to have gained a deeper insight into her situation and actually began seeing things more positively. Consequently, she was able to calmly discuss her feelings with her partner and work through their problems. She later thanked me for listening.

**Reflection**:
From this experience, I learned that just listening can be providing good customer care.

## 5. Have you been confronted by an aggressive customer?

### Evaluation

The ability to remain well-mannered and well-tempered while dealing with an aggressive customer is an absolute necessity. The recruiter will want to assess whether you can deal with confrontational issues in a calm and rational manner.

You will be assessed on how well you coped under the pressure and how you dealt with the customer. A good response will show that you never lost your temper and remained courteous throughout the experience.

### Sample Response

**Situation**:
Shortly after I began freelancing, I encountered a problem when an associate of mine tried to pressure me into a free service based on friendship.

**Action**:
I proceeded to offer her, what I considered to be, a reasonable discount, but she was not satisfied with my offer and proceeded to pressure me with emotional blackmail. I remained cordial, but became more assertive as I continued to refuse her demands.

**Result**:
Rather than accept the reasons for my decision, she became increasingly enraged, and even began to slander my service and friendship

Shocked at her over-reaction, and concerned about what might develop, I felt I had no option but to withdraw from the situation.

**Reflection**:
This experience was very challenging and certainly tested my patience. But I remained calm and, although this particular relationship never recovered, it was a learning experience that hasn't since been repeated.

# When have you had to say 'No' to a customer?

## Evaluation

There will be occasions when it is necessary to say no to a passenger. The recruiter wants to know that you aren't intimidated by such situations and have the strength of character to deal with the situation authoritatively, yet diplomatically.

You will be assessed on how you approached the customer and went about dealing with the situation. A good response will demonstrate your ability to use tact, and will show that you remained courteous throughout the experience.

## Sample Response

**Situation**:
I remember when a customer tried to return a pair of trainers to the store for a refund. Although the customer denied it, I could see that the shoes had clearly been worn.

**Action**:
I remained calm and polite as I suggested that the shoes could not be returned unless faulty or unused.

The customer become very aggressive and repeatedly threatened to contact our head office to complain about me if I didn't refund him immediately.

I remained assertive and suggested this would be the best course of action for him to take. I then proceeded to provide him with the full details of our complaints manager within the head office.

**Result**:
Realising defeat, the man stormed out of the shop and, to my knowledge, never did take the matter further.

## When have you handled a customer complaint?

> Evaluation
>
> The recruiter wants to know that you are able to retain your composure and use your problem solving skills when dealing with a dissatisfied customer.
>
> A good response will show that you never took the complaint personally, remained calm and courteous, and were able to create a satisfactory outcome for the customer.

### Sample Response

**Situation**:
I remember when a customer complained about a meal they had purchased.

Because over two thirds of the entire course had been eaten, not only was it obvious that the complaint was insincere, but it was also against the restaurants policy to offer a refund under such circumstances.

The customer was becoming very enraged and threatened to write to the trading standards and newspapers if I did not give him a full refund.

**Action**:
I gave the customer my undivided attention while he vented his frustrations. Then, when he had finally calmed down, I calmly apologised for the dissatisfaction and proceeded to offer a meal deal voucher as a goodwill gesture.

**Result**:
The customer was clearly unhappy not to have received a refund, but he left the restaurant and, as suspected, never did take the matter any further.

# 8. When have you had to resolve a conflict between what the customer wanted and what you could realistically deliver?

### Evaluation

The recruiter wants to determine that you have the strength of character to voice your concerns. They also want to see that you can be diplomatic, yet authoritative, in your communication style.

You will be assessed on how you approached the customer and how you dealt with the situation.

## Sample Response

**Situation**:
I remember a client who came to me for a colour treatment and restyle. She had used a virtual hairstyle software to create her ideal look and was beaming with excitement as she showed me the picture.

The style was notably very pretty, and it was clear that it was ideally suited to the client. Unfortunately, however, the client's hair had been through several perming and colour treatments, and the platinum blonde shade that she wanted just wasn't going to be possible at that time.

**Action**:
Knowing how excited the client was, I felt a little dejected as I proceeded to break this news to her. In the hope of relieving some of her obvious disappointment, I suggested a strand test to see if it would be possible to lift some of the colour without causing excessive damage. If the strand test were a success, we could perform a gradual transformation through the use of highlights.

**Result**:
Thankfully, the strand test was a success and the client, while naturally disappointed, was happy to go ahead with the gradual transformation. The result was striking, and the client was happy with the result.

Within nine months, the transformation was complete, and I had a very satisfied customer.

# 9 Describe a situation when the customer was wrong

> ### Evaluation
> Although the popular saying suggests otherwise, the customer isn't always right and the recruiter wants to know that you aren't Intimidated by such situations.
>
> You will be assessed on how you approached the customer and went about dealing the situation. A good response will demonstrate your ability to use tact, and will show that you remained courteous throughout the experience.

## Sample Response

**Situation**:
I remember a client who I had carried out a perming treatment for. After completing the treatment, I provided written instructions for how to care for her new perm which specifically instructed against washing the hair for at least 48 hours.

Unfortunately, the very next day the client washed her hair and the perm dropped out. The client was understandably very upset, but refused to accept that the perm had fallen out as a consequence of her own actions. She became very irate and started to slander my work and the salon.

**Action**:
When asked if she had followed the instructions, she denied being provided with any. I assured her that instructions were provided, and suggested she check her belongings.

**Result**:
Later that afternoon, the client returned to the salon holding onto the instruction sheet with a very embarrassed look on her face. She apologised profusely for her behaviour.

**Reflection**:
To avoid a repeat of this situation, I now provide clearer warnings within the written information sheet and back it up with verbal instructions.

# 10. Have you ever bent the rules for a customer?

## Evaluation

There are situations where it is permissible to bend the rules, however, some airlines may view rule bending very negatively. So, no matter how trivial or well-intended, you may want to play it safe and declare that you have never gone against the rules.

If you do decide to provide an answer, you should show that you are able to keep balance between company policy and the interest of customers.

## Sample Response

I have always abided by company policies and have never bent the rules. Bending the rules for one customer, will no doubt lead to a downward spiral . Either the customer will expect further rule bending, or other customers will catch on and expect the same treatment. It's just not a wise course of action to take.

## 11. Tell me about a time when you failed to communicate effectively?

### Evaluation

We all experience challenges in communication, but a complete failure to communicate effectively will show a lack of initiative and creativity in problem solving.

Whatever the reason for a communication challenge, there is always a way to communicate if you are willing to put in some additional effort. Your answer should reflect this.

### Sample Response (Modest Approach)

While I have certainly encountered communication challenges, I can honestly say that I have never yet completely failed in my ability to communicate. With some creativity, I have always found a way to overcome communication barriers.

### Sample Response (Humble Example)

**Situation:**
Generally, I am a very efficient communicator, but I do recall when I experienced difficulty communicating with an OAP client.

**Action:**
The client was very hard of hearing, and I tried everything to communicate with her. I spoke slower, louder, used hand gestures and facial expressions, I even tried to write the information down, but without her glasses she was unable see my writing clearly.

**Result:**
Fortunately, I managed to locate a magnifying glass, which enabled the client to read my instructions, and everything worked out well in the end.

# 12. When have your communication skills made a difference to a situation or outcome?

### Evaluation
The ability to communicate well is vital to the role of cabin crew, so you should have plenty of real life examples ready to share. This is your chance to shine, so don't be modest.

## Sample Response

**Situation**:
I remember a trainee apprentice we had in our department who never asked questions and refused all offers of help. Unfortunately, instead of trying to understand her reasons, everyone drew the conclusion that she was a know-it-all and vowed not to offer help in the future.

**Action**:
Concerned that her progress would suffer, I decided to offer my encouragement and support. It soon became evident from our conversation that she had excessively high expectations of herself and feared looking incompetent. I explained that it was okay to ask questions, and mistakes were expected. I even shared a few of my own early mishaps to lighten the mood.

**Result**:
Very quickly after that we saw a change in her behaviour. She began asking questions, she was more open to suggestions, and her skills improved immensely.

**Reflection**:
From this experience, I learnt that things are not always what they appear and we need to be more objective before making rash judgements.

## 13  Give an example of when you had to present complex information in a simplified manner in order to explain it to others

### Evaluation

As cabin crew, you may be required to break down and convey complex information to customers. For example, if a passenger is afraid of flying, you may need to explain the technicalities of the flight, or if a passenger is hasn't grasped the use of emergency equipment and emergency procedures, you may need to break the information down further.

Your answer here should show that you are able to express knowledge in a clear and simple manner.

### Sample Response

**Situation**:
I remember a client who was interested in having a colour treatment carried out. She was very inquisitive and asked numerous questions, so I could sense that she was concerned about the process and potential damage to her natural hair.

**Action**:
Not satisfied with a simple nontechnical version, I had to provide a detailed technical breakdown of the whole process. This involved describing the molecular structure of the hair, the effect colour particles have and how they bond to the structure.

**Result**:
Although I had to occasionally refer to training manuals to emphasise or clarify my point, overall the client was satisfied with my effort. As a direct result, she went ahead with the treatment and was very pleased with the outcome.

# 14. Have you ever had to overcome a language barrier?

> **Evaluation**
>
> As cabin crew, you will interact with a variety of people from a broad range of cultures and backgrounds. The ability to relate to others and adapt your communication style is, therefore, very important.

## Sample Response

**Situation**:
During a trip to Africa, I became acquainted with a French lady. She understood my French, the little amount I knew, but she didn't really understand English. Unfortunately, the amount of French I knew wasn't enough to get me through a whole conversation, so I had to improvise.

**Action**:
I spoke French wherever possible and filled in the gaps with improvised sign language and facial expressions.

**Result**:
At first it was a little tricky trying to find imaginative ways to communicate, but over time I became much more proficient. I'm sure she was amused by my amateur efforts, but it worked out well and I came away with a new friend.

**Reflection**:
Now when I encounter this type of communication barrier, I am much more confident in my ability to cope.

## 15 Tell me about a time that you had to work as part of a team

### Evaluation

The ability to work well within a team is absolutely essential to working as cabin crew. You should, therefore, have plenty of examples that demonstrate this ability.

Sample Response

**Situation**:
There was a particular time that stands out for me because it was such an unusual occurrence.

It was a usual quiet Tuesday afternoon and only myself, the senior stylist, an apprentice, and the salon manager were on duty. To our surprise, it was as if someone started offering out free chocolate, as clients started to filter through the doors.

**Action**:
Despite the overwhelming rush, we showed great teamwork as we pulled together and shared our duties. Even our manager showed great team spirit as she got involved with the hair service.

**Result**:
As a result of our teamwork, and some free relaxing conditioning treatments, we managed to deliver an outstanding service. Every client went away completely satisfied.

# 16. When have you struggled to fit in?

## Evaluation

With the constant rotation of crew, there will be some people that you don't immediately hit it off with. The recruiters want to know that you aren't intimidated by such difficulties and are able to move past any struggles.

## Sample Response

**Situation**:
When I started working at Trina's Hair & Beauty, I was joining a very close-knit team who had been together for a number of years.

As a result of the number of trainees they had witnessed come and go over the years, they had become a little reluctant to accept new trainees.

I wouldn't say it was a struggle to fit in as such, but I certainly experienced some growing pains. With remarks such as 'if you are still here then' to contend with, I knew I had to prove myself.

**Action**:
To show that I was serious about the job, and was not a fly-by-night, I focused a lot of effort on learning my new job. At the same time, I continued to be friendly and respectful of my new colleagues while I made a conscious effort to get to know them.

**Result**:
As a result of my hard effort, It didn't take long for them to accept me and include me as part of their team. Naturally, I have become closer to some of my colleagues than with others, but we all got on and worked well as a team.

# 17. Have you ever experienced difficulties getting along with colleagues?

## Evaluation

No matter how hard we try, or how likeable we are, there will always be someone that we don't hit it off with. To say otherwise, would not sound credible.

For the most part, this question is asked to determine your ability to get along with other people and manage adversity. The recruiters want to know that you don't allow conflict to interfere with work.

The best answer should show that you aren't intimidated or confrontational in such situations, but you put in the commitment necessary to build a respectful and healthy working relationship.

## Sample Response

**Situation**:
I remember one co-worker in particular who flat out didn't like me. It didn't matter what I did or said, or whether I tried to avoid or befriend this person.

**Action**:
After a couple of days of subtle hostility, I decided to assert myself. I diplomatically explained that I acknowledged her dislike for me and I asked for input as to what I must do to create a professional relationship

**Result**:
Although we never became friends, we were able to maintain more cordial relations thereafter.

# 18 Tell us about a challenge you have faced with a colleague

## Evaluation

Airlines have a constant rotation of crew on-board each aircraft and, especially within larger airlines, you may not work with the same crew members twice. As a result, it is guaranteed that you will encounter challenging situations with colleagues.

The recruiters want to know that you aren't intimidated by such colleagues or situations, and are prepared to use your initiative to diffuse or mediate as necessary to keep working relationships healthy.

Your answer should demonstrate your willingness to cooperate with others to resolve differences, improve relations, and manage conflicts. It should also display your ability to remain patient and positive in the face of adversity.

## Sample Response

**Situation**:
I do remember one situation where two of my colleagues really didn't hit it off with one another. They were constantly quarrelling and everyone had lost patience with them, but no one wanted to get involved.

**Action**:
In the end, I decided to take the initiative and act as a sort of mediator to the situation. I was not their manager, so I had to be as tactful as I could so that I wouldn't upset anyone.

I started by explaining that I acknowledged their dislike for each other and then I drew upon the fact that they are both professionals and can, therefore, put aside their differences for the good of the team.

**Result**:
They had a pretty frank discussion and, although I can't say they ended up the best of friends, they did work out an effective strategy for working more productively together.

# 19 Tell me about a disagreement with a colleague

### Evaluation

We all have disagreements with colleagues, but they should never get out of control or interfere with work.

You may choose to disclose the details of a conflict situation, but make sure it was minor and didn't interfere with work. Conversely, you may wish to play it safe and declare that while you have had disagreements, they were so minor that you don't really recall the exact details. You could then go on to reiterate some minor examples.

The recruiters want to know that you aren't intimidated by conflicts and have the ability to see things from another person's perspective. Your answer should demonstrate that you are prepared to use your initiative and interpersonal skills to improve relations with colleagues, even in cases where they cannot agree upon certain issues.

### Sample Response

**Introduction**:
Working in a creative environment with other highly skilled professionals, it was natural that we had the occassional clash of ideas. Any disagreements we did have, however, were so relatively minor and insignificant that I would be hard pressed to recall the exact details.

**Situation**:
Our disagreements were usually as a result of our individual preference towards certain products, styles, magazines or equipment.

**Action**:
Our debates were never confrontational and they never interfered with our work in any way.

**Result**:
In fact, some very interesting views emerged from these debates which sometimes resulted in people, including myself, having a slight change in my perspective. So, they were often very educational.

# 20 Have you successfully worked with a difficult coworker?

## Evaluation

The recruiters want to know that you aren't intimidated by difficult colleagues or situations, and are prepared to use your initiative to deal with the situation as necessary. You will be assessed on how you approached the colleague and how you dealt with the situation.

Your answer should demonstrate your willingness to co-operate with others to resolve differences, improve relations, and manage conflicts. It should also display your ability to remain patient and positive when challenging situations occur.

## Sample Response

**Situation**:
I remember one member of staff was always complaining. Nothing was ever good enough or couldn't possibly work. Everyone had lost patience with her but, because she was so incredibly sensitive, no one said anything.

**Action**:
I spent some time with her and tactfully told her that it appeared as if she was always putting our ideas down.

**Result**:
On hearing this feedback she was genuinely horrified at her own behaviour. She explained that she hadn't realised it had made everyone feel that way and agreed that from then on she would try to be more positive.

Very quickly after that we saw a change in her behaviour. She became more conscious of her own attitude and deliberately tried to be more considerate. From that point on, no one could have hoped for a more committed team member.

# Have you ever worked with someone you disliked?

## Evaluation

There will always be someone that we don't like and to try to convince the recruiter otherwise would not sound honest or credible.

For the most part, this question is asked to determine your ability to get along with other people and manage adversity. The recruiters want to know that you don't allow personal views cause conflict or interfere with work.

The best answer should show that you aren't intimidated or confrontational in such situations, but you put in the commitment necessary to build a respectful and healthy working relationship

## Sample Response

**Situation**:
There was one colleague I worked with that I really found it difficult to get along with personally.

**Action**:
Instead of focusing on those things I didn't like, I put my personal views aside and focused on the skills she brought to the position.

**Result**:
My personal view of her never changed, and we never became friends, but we did work productively alongside each other without any problems.

# 22 Have you ever acted as a mentor to a coworker?

## Evaluation

There may be times when you have to mentor new crew members and the recruiters are trying to assess your ability to lead and mentor your colleagues.

## Sample Response

**Situation**:
I remember when one of our trainees was having problems understanding certain aspects of her course material, and I could see she was becoming increasingly frustrated and self critical.

**Action**:
Having witnessed her in action, I knew that she was a very bright and talented individual with no obvious lack of skill. So, I determined that her frustrations were probably the result of the pressure she was feeling about her approaching exam.

Concerned at the effect this pressure was having on her, and having experienced the same pressures myself, I decided to offer my support. To reinforce her understanding, I demonstrated some of the techniques she had been struggling with and showed her a few memory tips and tricks which had helped me through my exams.

**Result**:
My breakdown of the processes, along with the visual demonstration I provided, seemed to make the material much more understandable for her. In the days that followed, she seemed to have a new lease of life and was much more positive. Subsequently, she passed her exams with top grades.

# 23 What have you done that shows initiative?

## Evaluation

Your answer here should show that you take the initiative when it comes to additional work and demonstrate a natural desire for doing extra tasks willingly.

### Sample Response

**Situation**:
When I began working for my current employer, the inventory system was outdated and the storage room was very messy and disorganised.

**Action**:
I came in on my day off, cleaned up the mess, organised the store cupboards and catalogued it all on the new inventory forms.

**Result**:
Thereafter, when orders arrived it was easy to organise and retrieve.

**Reflection**:
If I'm able to do the task, instead of waiting for the job to be done, I simply do it.

# 24. Have you undertaken a course of study, on your own initiative, in order to improve your work performance?

## Evaluation

Your answer here should show that you are committed to self-development and take the initiative when it comes to improving yourself and your efficiency.

## Sample Response

**Situation**:
While at Trina's Hair Salon, we were experiencing a spectacular rise in demand for high fashion cuts. I had some creative cutting experience, but nothing that extended to the kind of advanced skill that was required for true high fashion cuts.

**Action**:
After some consideration, I decided that increasing my creative cutting skills would not only give the salon a competitive advantage, but it would also be a fantastic opportunity for me to move my skills to the next level. So, I took the initiative and, under my own funding, immediately enrolled onto a creative cutting course.

**Result**:
My new skills proved to be an instant success. Existing clients began recommending me to their friends, which resulted in a massive rise in clientele. Needless to say, my manager was very happy.

# 25. Describe an improvement that you personally initiated

### Evaluation

The recruiter wants to know that you seek better and more effective ways of carrying out your work and can suggest improvements that will achieve more efficiency.

Your answer here should show that you take the initiative when it comes to improving working methods and standards.

### Sample Response

**Situation**:
While travelling in India, I learnt the art of Indian head massage.

**Action**:
When I returned to work, I began using my new skill on clients while carrying out the shampoo.

**Result**:
My massages were becoming such a success, that my manager approached me to request that I train my colleagues. Naturally, I was honoured to oblige.

# 26 Describe a new idea or suggestion that you made to your supervisor

### Evaluation
The recruiter wants to know that you aren't afraid to take the initiative and suggest improvements.

### Sample Response

**Situation**:
When I was working at Trina's Hair Salon, I had noticed that a lot of our clients wore nail extensions.

**Action**:
Convinced that the service would be an improvement to our already successful salon, I carried out extensive independent research before presenting the idea to my manager.

**Result**:
After carrying out her own research, she liked the idea so much that she decided to go ahead with the new service. Within a couple of months, the service was up and running, and we experienced a dramatic increase in new clientele and revenue. I even got a small bonus in my pay packet for my involvement.

# 27 Tell me about a problem you encountered and the steps you took to overcome it

### Evaluation

The recruiter will be assessing how well you cope with diverse situations, and how you use your judgment and initiative to solve problems.

In answering this question, you need to provide a concrete example of a problem you faced, and then Itemize the steps you took to solve the problem. Your answer should demonstrate a patient and positive attitude towards problem solving.

## Sample Response

**Situation**:
Early in my freelancing career, I experienced several clients who turned up late to their appointments. Some even forgot about their appointments altogether. Rather than just simply being an inconvenience, it was wasting my time and money.

**Action**:
I considered my options and decided that the best solution would be to send out reminder cards a few days prior to client appointments. For the repeat offenders, I would enforce a late cancellation fee.

**Result**:
This decision drastically cut the number of late arrivers, and I have never since had a no-show.

# 28 Tell me about a problem that didn't work out

## Evaluation

No matter how hard we try, there are some instances where a problem just doesn't work out. To say otherwise will not sound honest or credible.

In answering this question, you need to first ensure that the problem was a minor one which had no negative or lasting impact on the company, a colleague or a customer. Try to accentuate the positives and keep your answer specific. Itemize the steps you took to deal with the problem and make it clear that you learnt from the experience.

## Sample Response

**Situation**:
Shortly after I began freelancing, my bank returned a client's cheque to me through lack of funds.

**Action**:
At first, I was sure it was a mistake caused through an oversight on the part of my client. I made a number of calls, left several messages and even attempted a visit to the clients home, all to no avail.

Several weeks passed and it was clear that I was chasing a lost cause. At this point, I had to decide whether to write off the debt and blacklist the client or visit the Citizens' Advice for advice on retrieving the funds.

**Result**:
After careful consideration of all the factors involved, I decided to write the debt off as a learning experience.

**Reflection**:
In hindsight, I realise it was a silly mistake that could easily have been avoided. I have never repeated this error since as I now wait for the funds to clear before carrying out a service.

# 29 Have you ever taken the initiative to solve a problem that was above your responsibilities?

## Evaluation

Those candidates who demonstrate that they use their initiative and put in extra effort to provide a better and more complete service will surely be looked upon favourably.

## Sample Response

**Situation**:
It had been quite an uneventful afternoon when, all of the sudden, in walked an obviously frantic customer.

From what I could understand, her laptop had contracted a virus while connected to the internet and the system now failed to respond to any commands.

Being a self-employed web designer, the customer was naturally very concerned about the potential loss of data, and earnings.

Unfortunately, while the laptop was still within warranty, it was beyond the companies scope and had to be sent to the manufacturer for restoration. My colleagues, while polite, but could only offer assistance as far as sending the laptop to the manufacturer.

**Action**:
I could sense the customer was becoming increasingly distressed and, having had previous training in system restoration, I was confident that I could at least safely extract the data from the hard drive.

After talking the customer through the procedure, she granted her permission and I proceeded.

**Result**:
After some 45 minutes of fiddling with wires and hard drives, the customer's data had been successfully, and safely, extracted. The customer gasped a big sigh of relief as we packaged the laptop off to the manufacturer for repair.

Several weeks later, my line manager received a letter from the customer complimenting my efforts.

**Reflection**:
I was really pleased that a little effort made such a big difference.

# 30. When have you made a bad decision?

### Evaluation

We all make decisions that we regret, and to say otherwise will not sound honest or credible.

The recruiter will be assessing whether you have the character to admit and take responsibility for your mistake, whether your decision had a negative impact on customers or the company, and whether you learnt from this mistake?

In answering this question, you need to first ensure that the mistake was a minor one, which had no negative or lasting impact on the company, a colleague or a customer. Try to accentuate the positives and keep your answer specific. Itemize what you did and how you did it. Finally, you need to make it clear that you leant from the mistake and will be certain not to repeat it.

**Situation**:

Early in my freelance career, I was approached by a salesman who was promoting a protein conditioning system. He described the system as "The newest technology to emerge from years of research. Guaranteed to help heal, strengthen, and protect".

Although I was excited by the concept, I did have my concerns that the system sounded too good to be true. However, the salesman had all the official paperwork to back up his claims, and the literature was thorough and well presented. All these things, combined with the company's full money-back guarantee, made it appear to be a win-win situation, and a risk worth taking. So I invested.

Following my investment, I decided to test the system out on training heads before taking the system public. Unfortunately, several months of using the system passed with no obvious benefits.

**Action**:
Disappointed with the product, I decided to pursue the full money back guarantee, but the sales number was not recognised, and my letters were returned unopened. Even their website had mysteriously vanished. I soon came to the realisation that I had been taken in by an elaborate scam.

I contacted the Citizens Advice Bureau and Trading Standards, but there was little they could do to retrieve my funds.

**Result**:
Unfortunately, I never recovered my costs and had to put the mistake down to a learning experience.

**Reflection**:
Unfortunately, it really was my fault. I should have trusted my gut instinct and carried out thorough research before making my decision. It is a mistake I shall never repeat.

# 31 What was the biggest challenge you have faced?

## Evaluation

In answering this question, you need to provide a concrete example of a challenge you faced, and then Itemize the steps you took to overcome that challenge.

Your answer should display a patient and positive attitude when challenging situations occur.

## Sample Response

**Situation**:
To be honest, giving up smoking was the biggest challenge. I never thought I could do it, and I had made dozens of attempts that ended in failure.

**Action**:
Determined not to give in to my withdrawals, I decided I needed an incentive that would pull me through the tough times. Being sponsored for a worthy cause was the perfect solution.

**Result**:
With a good cause in mind, the following three months were easier than on previous occasions. Not only have I come out the other end a non-smoker, I also managed to raise £2464.00 for Childline.

**Reflection**:
Since I gave up smoking, I have gained so much personal insight, and I deal with potentially stressful situations at work so much more effectively now, I feel more energetic, more mentally alert and far calmer now than I ever did before.

> "I sometimes find that in interviews you learn more about yourself than the person learned about you."
>
> *- William Shatner*

# SAMPLE ANSWERS
## FOR TRADITIONAL QUESTIONS

# Cabin Crew

## What do you know about the job?

"I know that the service we see as passenger's form only a small portion of what actually goes on in the job. With safety being the primary concern, there are procedures and checks which must be constantly and consistently completed. Then, when things go wrong, cabin crew are there to take control. Moreover, it is a constant process of cleaning and preparation, paperwork and stock checks, tending to passenger comfort and being of service. Clearly the profession is a very demanding one, but it is also a very exciting and fulfilling one for the right person, which I do believe I am."

## Do you think the role of cabin crew is glamorous?

"Having thoroughly researched the position, I am aware that the glamour associated with the role is rather superficial. Sure there are benefits of travel, and the crew certainly do make themselves appear glamorous, but the constant travelling between time zones, the long and tiring shifts, unpredictable schedules and irregular working patterns place tough demands on crew and make the job anything but glamorous."

## What do you think are the advantages of this position?

"The randomness and variety of the different crew, passenger profiles, roster structure and destinations excite me greatly. They are unique elements that you just don't find in normal nine to five jobs. It's a job I will find rewarding in a number of ways."

## What do you think are the disadvantages?

"The obvious disadvantages are the flight delays and cancellations that crew experience. While passengers also experience these issues, crew experience those far more often. This makes for very long and tiring shifts, irregular working patterns and unpredictable schedules.

Moreover, the regular crossing between different time zones can take its toll leading to jet lag and fatigue. Ultimately, though, these challenges are part of the job and, with some advance preparation, they can be managed to a certain degree."

### Avoid sounding naive

To deny the obvious drawbacks of the job will only make you sound naive and unprepared. So, be up front about the disadvantages and demonstrate that you have considered these carefully.

## What would you change about this position?

"By applying for this position, I have accepted everything that comes with it. I see no point in concerning myself about those things that cannot be changed."

## What aspects of customer service are most important to our passengers?

"Passengers want to feel comfortable and looked after by the airline and crew. They want to be assured that crew will listen to and answer their questions, and will be friendly and polite in doing so. If crew are not approachable, passengers feel unwelcome and unsure."

## What do you think contributes to passenger frustrations?

"Feeling tired from travelling can cause passengers to feel unusually frustrated. Add to this flight delays, long waiting times and space constrictions, and frustration naturally increases. If the passenger is then greeted by seemingly unwelcoming staff, their tension will certainly rise much further."

## Why do you think some passengers vent their frustrations on cabin crew?

"In the first instance, cabin crew wear the airline's uniform. Thus, passengers consider them to be a representative of the airline. Moreover, the passengers spend more time with cabin crew than with any other member of the airline staff, so they simply become an easy target."

## What contribution can you make to ensure passengers will fly with us again?

My customer service experience and friendly character style will enable me to deliver a superior standard of service which will make passengers feel welcome, valued and relaxed.

## Why should we hire you instead of someone with cabin crew experience?

"Although I might not have cabin crew experience, I have the necessary skills to make an impressive start, and the willingness to learn and improve. Sometimes, employers do better when they hire people who don't have a great deal of repetitive experience. That way, they can train these employees in their methods and ways of doing the job. Training is much easier than untraining."

## Why should we hire you for this position rather than another applicant?

"I can't tell you why you should hire me instead of another candidate but, I can tell you why you should hire me."

## Are you willing to start as a trainee?

"Yes, absolutely. This is a new area for me, and I believe in getting a good foundation in the basics before progressing. An entry level position will enable me to learn the position inside out, and will give me the opportunity to grow when I prove myself. I also have a great deal of knowledge and work experience, which I'm sure will contribute to my successful progression through training."

## How do you feel about the probationary period?

"I can see no problem with a probationary period. I am a fast learner so it shouldn't take me long to prove myself."

## How do you feel about working at Christmas, and other special occasions?

"Naturally, I would miss spending time with my friends and family, but my career is important to me and my family and friends respect and appreciate that fact. I am happy to make the sacrifice as necessary."

## How do you feel about a formal dress code?

"I have always liked to dress formally and feel very comfortable wearing formal attire. I realise that a standard of dress is necessary in order to project a professional image to the passengers."

## This is a long hours culture, is that a problem for you?

"I understand that this a demanding job, but I really do thrive on the challenge of this sort of work and have worked long hours in the past, so I am willing to work whatever hours are necessary to get the work done."

## This position will involve relocating, how will you adjust to the different lifestyle?

"I realise that this position involves transfers, and I bore that in mind when I applied. I am fully aware of what to expect from the research I have done and would welcome the different lifestyle."

## How do you feel about the routine tasks and irregular hours of this job?

"I accept that every role carries with it a certain amount of routine in order to get the job done. If my job involves repetitive work, it is my responsibility to carry it out to the best of my abilities. As for irregular hours I would expect to have an indication of my core hours, but will work the hours that are necessary in order to fulfil the requirements of the role."

## Do you feel confident in your ability to handle this position?

"Yes, absolutely. I'm very confident in my abilities. I'm familiar with the basic job requirements and I learn quickly. It undoubtedly will take time and effort on my part, but I'm more than willing to devote that time and effort."

## Do you feel ready for a more responsible position?

"Absolutely. I believe that eight years experience working closely with customers, has prepared me professionally and personally to move up to this role. My customer care and teamwork skills have been finely tuned over the years, and I know I am capable of greater achievements."

## How will you cope with the change in environment?

"I welcome the challenge of learning about and adapting to a new environment, that's one of the reasons I'm seeking to make a career change right now. Any major change, while always containing some challenge is a chance to grow, learn, and advance."

# The Airline

## Have you ever flown with us?

"Yes, I have had the fortunate opportunity to fly with Fly High Airlines on several occasions now. With the attentive crew, outstanding meal service and comfortable seating, I always feel as though I am flying first class. I am now a frequent flyer and very happy customer. I now hope to join your team in providing this fantastic service."

## How would you rate us against our competitors?

Example 1
"It's so difficult to be objective, and I really don't like to slight your competition."

Example 2
"My experiences with each of the airlines I have flown with have all been good, and I never had a problem or cause for complaint. An advantage of Fly High Airlines, however, is the attentiveness of the crew. They really take care of all their passengers and do everything to make the flight as pleasant as possible. I have always been made to feel welcome on board your flights."

## Do you think we have a good reputation?

"Absolutely! Through my own experience, I have encountered attentive and efficient crew, fantastic meals and comfortable seating. In researching the airline, it appears that others agree with these observations.

The variety of awards the airline has received over the years is a sure testament to its fantastic reputation."

## What is the worst thing you have heard about us?

"The worst thing I have heard about Fly High Airlines is that competition for jobs is fierce because it is such a terrific airline. Everything else I have heard, have been overly positive."

## Is there anything you think we do badly?

"In conducting my research into the airline, I haven't come across anything to suggest that you are doing anything badly. In fact, I have discovered quite the opposite.

Plus, I am sure you wouldn't enjoy your current success and be receiving so many awards for excellence if you were doing anything really wrong."

## How do you feel about working for a small airline?

"I have always valued the feeling of a small company. They haven't become large and impersonal and I like the potential for being involved in the growth of the airline."

### How do you feel about working for a large airline?

"I welcome the opportunity to work in a large, developed and well known airline such as this. The resources and potential for advancement are not available in smaller airlines. I'd be proud to apply my skills and abilities to the excellence that flourishes here."

### Have you applied to any other airlines?

"Although it is taking a bit of a risk, I haven't applied to other airlines because I am set on working for you. I wanted to see how my application went with you before I considered other options."

### If another airline offered you a job, would you take it?

"Because I am set on making cabin crew my future career, if I did not get this job with you, then I would have to consider other airlines. However, Fly High Airlines are at the very top of my list and I would be naturally disappointed not to get the job with you."

# Career History

## Why did you leave your last job?

» No opportunities
"While I enjoyed working for my previous employer, and appreciate the skills I developed while I was there, I felt I was not being challenged enough in the job. After working my way up through the company, there were no further opportunities for advancement."

» Redundancy
"I survived the first layoffs, but unfortunately this one got me."

» Temporary position
"The job was only a temporary position which I took to broaden my experience."

## Why have you had so many jobs?

» Broaden experience
"I wanted to experience different jobs to broaden my knowledge, skills and experience. This has provided me with a very valuable and rounded skill set."

» Temporary positions
"Due to the lack of full time opportunities in my area, I was only able to secure short term contracts."

» Youth
In my youth, I was unsure about the direction I wanted to take in my career. I have matured a great deal since those days and am now interested in establishing myself into a long term opportunity.

## Why were you fired?

The recruiters will not care if a termination was unjust, unfair or has a good explanation, a termination is a big red flag and will mark the end of your interview so you need to do everything you can to avoid disclosing it.

If you do decide that honesty is the best policy for you, then here are some tips to help you lighten the blow.

- Incompatibility
  "I was desperate for work and took the job without fully understanding the expectations. It turned out that my competencies were not a right match for the employer's needs so we agreed that it was time for me to move on to a position that would be more suitable. I certainly learnt a great deal from this experience, and it's not a mistake I will ever repeat."

- Personal reasons
  "I had been going through a rough patch in my personal life which, unfortunately, upset my work life. It is regrettable and my circumstances have now changed, but I really wasn't in the position to avoid it at the time"

Never:
- Badmouth previous employers, colleagues or bosses.
- Place blame
- Tell lies
- Reveal team incompatibility

## Why were you unemployed for so long?

- » Study
  "I wanted to broaden my knowledge base, so I went back into full time study."

- » Travel
  "I wanted to experience the world before settling into a long term career. I am now well travelled and ready to commit."

- » Youth
  "In my youth, I felt confused about the direction I wanted my career to take. I am now much more mature and certain in my desired direction."

- » Personal reasons
  "Personal circumstances prohibited me from taking gainful employment, however, circumstances have now changed and I am ready to get back to work."

It is better to say that you chose to take time off between jobs than it is to give the impression that you were unemployable.

## Why did you stay with the same employer for so long?

"I was there for several years, but in a variety of different roles. The opportunities for growth were fantastic so it felt as though I was undergoing frequent changes without actually changing employer. I didn't see the need to move on."

## Why have you decided to change professions at this stage of your career?

"This career turnaround hasn't come suddenly. I have always wanted to become cabin crew and have been gradually mastering the skills needed to perform its tasks. I have now reached a point in my life where I am prepared to make the career and lifestyle change. I want to take advantage of that opportunity while it is presented to me."

## What do you like about your current job?

"Rather than pick out the little details of the routine work, here are three general things. First is customer satisfaction. Seeing a client's face glow with happiness when their hair is transformed gives me an intense feeling of pride. Second is the interaction I get with my colleagues and clients. Finally, I enjoy being creative and finding new ways to please the customer."

## Which particular aspect of your work do you find most frustrating?

"That's an interesting question because I am, generally speaking, a tolerant person. Slow periods can be sources of frustration, but at times like that I put more effort into advertising and establishing new clientele. That way, the slow periods don't last long."

# Character Traits

## Are you an introvert or extrovert?

"Actually, I would describe myself as an ambivert because I enjoy social interaction, but am equally happy to spend time alone in my own company."

## What makes you stand out from the crowd?

"My friendly and positive nature certainly defines me as a person and makes me stand out from the crowd. I adopt a very optimistic view in every aspect of my life and refuse to allow external circumstances to negatively affect my state."

## If you had to characterise yourself in one sentence, what would you say?

"I am a friendly and approachable person, who is sincere and very optimistic about life."

## Rate yourself on a scale from 1 to 10

"I would rate myself as an 8. I always give my best, but in doing so I increase my skills. I, therefore, always see room for improvement."

## How would a friend describe you?

"My friends would describe me as sociable, cheerful and optimistic. They would also say I am someone who thinks fast on my feet and stays calm in adverse situations."

## How would an enemy describe your character?

"I suppose they might say that I am tenacious because I don't give in without a struggle, but am realistic about my limits. They might say I am brave because I am prepared to confront issues when there is a need, but I weigh the consequences and don't act irresponsibly. And, maybe, driven because I push for what I want, but can back off when advisable to do so."

## How have you changed in the last five years?

"I feel like I have matured rather than aged five years. The skills I have acquired and the qualities I have developed have changed me enormously, and I know there are parts of me that are still not being utilised half as effectively as they could be. My customer care and communication skills have definitely been improved, and I have a better ability to use my initiative and think on my feet."

# Customer Focus

## How would you define good customer service?

"Good customer service is about constantly and consistently meeting customer's expectations by providing a friendly, efficient and reliable service throughout the life of the service and/or product.

Excellent customer service is about exceeding customer's expectations by going beyond the call of duty. I believe that because no two customers are the same, they deserve to receive a service that is tailored to their individual needs. This is where a service moves beyond being just a satisfactory one, and becomes an excellent one."

## What do you think constitutes poor customer service?

"Poor service is when customers are treated with disrespect and provided with a poor quality product and/or service by rude, ignorant and unhelpful staff."

## Do you think the customer is always right?

"Whilst every customer is important, they are certainly not always right. Those who exhibit abusive behaviour, or do anything to compromise safety are straying beyond the boundary."

## When have you witnessed good customer service?

"I remember when I visited a local restaurant for a luncheon. It had just turned 3pm on a Wednesday afternoon and, much to mine and the management's surprise, they were exceptionally busy with only three waiting staff on duty. Despite the overwhelming rush our waitress, Claire, was very polite and helpful. The staff showed great teamwork as they managed to pull together and deliver an outstanding service."

## When have you witnessed poor customer service?

"I needed a particular material for a dress I was making. In most stores the salesperson would give me a quick 'no' before I finished explaining what I was looking for. I hadn't really noticed until I experienced the opposite service in another smaller fabric store."

## What do you enjoy about providing customer care?

"The most enjoyable aspect I would have to say is that because I genuinely care about my client's satisfaction, it rewards me personally when I know that they are happy with the job I did. This, in turn, drives me to do better."

## What do you dislike about providing customer care?

"Providing good customer care can be a challenge, and some people may view that negatively, but I view each challenge as an opportunity to develop and grow. So, because I am committed to developing myself, I welcome and enjoy the challenges of providing customer care. It is something I have become very good at."

## What do you find most challenging about providing customer service?

"Providing customer service is a challenge in itself. Because people are unpredictable by their very nature, you have to always expect the unexpected and be prepared to go beyond the call of duty and deal with issues as they arrive."

# Team Spirit

## How would you define teamwork?

"Teamwork is a group of people who work cooperatively together to achieve a common goal. They make a coordinated effort and each individual contributes their unique skills and ideas to the task."

## Do you prefer to work alone or as part of a team?

"I am happy either way, and equally efficient at both. So, whether I prefer to work alone or in a team would depend on the best way to complete the job.

I do, however, have a preference towards team spirit. As well as the interaction, there is greater satisfaction when you share the joy of completing a task."

## Are you a team player?

"Absolutely I am. As you will have observed during the group assessments, I interact well with others, and readily adapt to new people. I am a good listener, I respect other people's opinions and I can be relied on to contribute to the overall goal.

In fact, my previous supervisor used to say that my infectious optimism created excitement in other team members and resulted in a greater team effort and higher output."

## What role do you assume in a team situation?

"I am whatever I need to be. If a situation comes up and someone needs to take charge, then I will. But if someone else has already taken charge and is solving it, I will follow their lead."

## What do you enjoy about working as part of a team?

"There's nothing like being part of a great team where you can learn from the other members, bounce ideas off one another, and share achievements and rewards. There is a unique feeling of camaraderie that can never be experienced from working alone."

## What do you least enjoy about working as part of a team?

"People not pulling their weight can be frustrating. However, I've noticed that such people simply lack enthusiasm or confidence, and that energetic and cheerful coworkers can often change that."

## What do you find most challenging about being part of a team?

"The most challenging aspect is inspiring and motivating other team members. Each has different needs and is motivated by different things."

## Are you happy to be supervised by people who are younger than yourself?

"Absolutely. I don't consider age to be an important factor. What matters is a person's credibility, professionalism and competency."

# Communication

## What is the importance of having good communication skills?

"The ability to speak clearly, listen actively and comprehend effectively is vital for our successful interaction with others, and continued growth."

## How confident are you about addressing a group?

"I used to be nervous about speaking in front of a group, yet I found that preparation, practice and knowing my subject helped me overcome this, I now have no problem addressing a group."

## Rate your communication skills on a scale of 1 to 10.

"I would rate myself as an 8. I always give my best, but in doing so I increase my skills. I, therefore, always see room for improvement."

## Do you think your lack of language skills will affect your ability to perform the job?

"I admit my language skills are a little light, however, I am working on increasing my language fluency and, should I be offered the position, I will be sure to work on increasing my language abilities even further."

# Hypothetical

Hypothetical questions present candidates with difficult real-life situations, where almost any answer can be challenged.

A good way to approach these questions is to consider the feelings of everyone involved, and think about the implications for your colleagues and the airline.

Prove to the recruiters that you would be proactive and do your best to resolve the situation using your own initiative, whilst remembering that you could ask for the help of the more experienced crew if necessary.

If you have followed these guidelines and are still challenged, the recruiter may be testing your ability to manage conflict or stress. Bear in mind that if you are not cabin crew yet, you cannot really be expected to know the best reply so do not be tricked into entering into an argument with the recruiter.

In either case it is important to remain calm and focused, and to demonstrate that, although you appreciate there are many aspects to each situation, you would always be trying to find acceptable solutions.

If you really can't think of a solution, you can simply say, "That is a new area for me so I am afraid I can't really answer that, but I enjoy acquiring new knowledge and I do learn quickly."

## You are in flight at 30,000 feet. How would you handle a passenger if he became irate about his lost baggage?

"At 30,000 feet, there is not a lot you can do about the baggage, so the problem at hand is reassuring the passenger and avoiding further disruption.

First, I would try to manoeuvre the passenger somewhere more private where they can explain the situation. I would then apologise for the mishandling, and offer to assist on the ground by escorting him to the proper people who can help."

## What would you do if the seat belt signs are on due to turbulence, but a passenger gets up to go to the toilet?

"Because of the importance of passenger safety, I would advise the passenger to wait until the seat belt signs have been turned off. If the passenger really cannot wait, I will follow the corporate policy for dealing with such a situation."

## How would you handle a passenger who is intoxicated?

"I would not provide any more alcoholic beverages. I would encourage food, and offer a cup of tea or coffee. If the situation worsens beyond my control, I would inform my senior and seek assistance from the other crew members."

### What would you do if a commercially important passenger complained about a crying child?

"I would apologise to the passenger and offer my assistance to the guardian of the child."

### How would you deal with a passenger who is scared of flying?

"Being aware of what to expect, and just realising that a plane's wings are supposed to flex and move around gently in flight, can help relieve anxiety. Similarly, the collection of bumps and bangs that always accompany a flight can be made less fearsome if they are expected. So, I would try to comfort the passenger by talking them through the flight, and reassuring them of any strange noises they may hear.

I would advise them where I can be found, and show them the call bell. I would then check on them periodically throughout the flight."

### How would you deal with a passenger who is not right but believes he is right?

"I would explain the company's rules and policies to the passenger in a calm, professional and positive manner. Hopefully, this should clarify any misconceptions that the passenger may have."

### How would you handle a colleague who is being rude or racist?

"I would act immediately to put a stop to any racist or rude behaviour by making it clear to the person that their behaviour is not acceptable. If he or she continues, I would then report it to proper authority."

### If you spotted a colleague doing something unethical or illegal, what would you do?

"I would act immediately to put a stop to any unethical or illegal activity. I would try to document the details of the incident and try to collect any physical evidence. Then I would report it to my senior."

### What would you do if you suspect that a passenger is suspicious or a high risk to passengers?

"I would keep watch before reporting to the senior any abnormal behaviour indicating a suspicious passenger."

### What would you do and how would you react in a hijacking?

"I would remain calm, and follow the emergency guidelines and procedures."

### How would you act in an emergency such as a crash landing?

"As soon as I get the warning that something is going to happen, I would get a plan together in my mind. I would stay calm and in control and follow the emergency guidelines and procedures."

### What three items would you choose to have if trapped on a desert island?

"The three items I would have to have would be a medical kit containing various items such as medicines, water purification tablets, surgical blades, plasters and cotton wool. Second, I would have my survival kit containing essential items such as a compass, a striker and flint, torch, waterproof matches, a magnifying glass, and fish hooks and line. Third, a good survival guidebook."

### If you were trapped on a desert island, what book would you want?

"I would have to have an SAS survival guide."

### If you were going to Mars, what three items would you take?

"First, I would take a trained astronaut. Second, sufficient food for the journey and finally, enough fuel for the return trip."

# Adverse

### Have you stretched the truth today to gain a favourable outcome?

"Absolutely not. I haven't tried to be someone I am not, because I wouldn't want to get the job that way. To do so would be such a short term gain because eventually I would be found out."

### How would you respond if we told you that you have been unsuccessful on this occasion?

"Naturally, I will be a disappointed if I do not secure this job with you because it is something I really want, I feel ready for it, and I have had plenty to contribute. However, I am not one to give up quickly. I will think about where I went wrong and how I could have done better, and I would then take steps towards strengthening my candidacy."

### What would you say if I said your skills and experience were below the requirements of this job?

"I would ask what particular aspects of my skills and experience you felt were lacking and address each one of those areas with examples of where my skills and experiences do match your requirements. I would expect that after this discussion you would be left in no doubt about my ability to do this job."

## Aren't you overqualified for this position?

"I wouldn't say that I am overqualified, but certainly fully qualified. With more than the minimal experience, I offer immediate returns on your investment. Don't you want a winner with the skill sets and attitudes to do just that?"

## What question could I ask that would intimidate you?

"I can't think of any question that would intimidate me. This is probably the most intimidating question."

## How would you rate me as a recruiter?

"First, I'd give you high marks for your people skills. You helped me feel at ease right away, which made it easier for me to answer the questions. I'd also rate you highly on the creativity of the questions, and their thoroughness. By probing me as carefully as you have, you've given me a better opportunity to secure this position. You've given me a complete picture of what to expect at Fly High Airlines, and it confirms my belief that this is where I want to work."

## I'm not sure you are suitable for the position. Convince me.

"I am absolutely suitable. In fact, I am confident that I am perfect for this position.

You are looking for someone who is customer focused. Well, as you can see from my résumé, I have worked in client facing roles for eight years so have had plenty of experience dealing with the various aspects. I also run a successful business that relies on customer satisfaction. The fact that I am still in business, and have a solid and increasing client base, is a clear testament to my abilities.

Furthermore, you need someone who has a calm approach, and retains their composure in the face of adversity. Again, I have demonstrated this capability on several occasions throughout my career.

Beyond this, I have a friendly and optimistic character. I am hard working, I thrive on challenges and will always strive to deliver the highest standard of service to your passengers.

I am confident that my skills, experience and personal qualities will complement your existing team and allow me to make a positive contribution to the airline's ongoing success."

## Do you work well under pressure?

"Absolutely. Because pressure is the result of a new challenge, I perceive pressure as an opportunity to develop and grow. The more challenges I experience, the better my skills become, and the less I feel the pressure of subsequent challenges. So, because I am committed to developing myself, I welcome the challenges of pressure."

### How would I know you were under pressure?

"I disguise my pressure well, therefore, I would hope that it wouldn't be obvious enough to notice."

### What types of people annoy you or try your patience?

"That's an interesting question, because I am a very tolerant person. However, there are instances where my patience is put to the test, but I am able to control myself and my emotions, so I never let my patience move beyond the testing stage."

### Do you have difficulties tolerating people with different views than you?

"No. I recognise that everyone has their own views, and that they may not always correspond with my own. Differing views and personalities are what make us individual, so I don't let other people's views or interests affect how I feel about them."

### How often do you lose your temper?

"I never lose my temper. I regard that sort of behaviour as counterproductive and inappropriate. By losing your temper, you cannot possibly resolve a problem. Even if you're completely right, losing your temper often destroys your ability to convince others of this."

## What makes you angry or impatient?

"Anger to me means loss of control, and I'm not the kind of person who loses control. It is counterproductive and inappropriate, and doesn't gain anything of value.

When I feel stress building up, instead of getting angry or impatient, I take a deep breath and begin to focus on the positives. The results are quite dramatic, my whole demeanour changes very rapidly,"

## How do you handle criticism?

"As long as the criticism is fair and constructive, I listen to it and remain gracious. I thank them for their candid feedback, express regret over the situation and modify my future behaviour accordingly."

# Closing

## So you do still wish us to consider you for this position?

"Absolutely! Having had this chance to meet you and learn more about the airline and position, I am even more eager than before. I am convinced that this is the opportunity I am seeking, and I know I can make a positive contribution."

## Would you take this job if we offered it to you?

"Yes, definitely. I was eager as soon as I saw the job opening on your web site. More than that though, actually meeting potential colleagues and finding out more about the airline and the position has clarified still further what an exciting challenge it would be to work here."

## When are you available to start if offered the position?

"I have the energy and enthusiasm to start straight away. All I need is a week's notice and I'm ready."

## Where do you picture yourself in five years?

"I very much hope that I shall be with Fly High Airlines in five years time. By which time, I will have made a significant contribution to the airline, will have become an experienced senior member of the cabin crew team, and will be working on new ways to advance my career further."

### If offered the job, how long will you stay with us?

"I'm approaching this job with a long term view. I hope to make enough of a contribution the airline, that I can move up through the ranks to become an experienced senior member of the cabin crew team."

### Do you have any reservations about working here?

"I don't have any reservations at this point. I see this position as a fine opportunity, and the airline as one I would be proud to be an employee of."

### Can we contact previous employers for references?

"Yes, absolutely. I'm confident that all my references will be favourable and will confirm what we've discussed here today."

> "Choose a job you love, and you will never have to work a day in your life"
>
> *- Confucius*

# ASK THE RIGHT QUESTIONS

# Ask the RIGHT QUESTIONS

This section of the interview is a real chance for you to shine and set yourself apart from all the other candidates. Therefore, it is a good idea to prepare one or two intelligent questions in advance.

The questions you ask, and how you ask them, say a lot about you, your motives, your depth of knowledge about the airline and the position itself.

## Guidelines

The questions you ask should follow these guidelines:

- » Don't ask questions that could be easily answered through your own research.
- » Ask questions which demonstrate a genuine interest in and knowledge of the airline and the position.
- » Demonstrate that you know just that little bit more than is required.

## Question About Suitability

Asking recruiters to raise their concerns about your suitability will provide you with an opportunity to follow up and reassure the recruiter.

- » Do you have any reservations about my ability to do this job?
- » What do you foresee as possible obstacles or problems I might have?
- » Is there anything else I need to do to maximise my chances of getting this job?
- » How does my background compare with others you have interviewed?
- » Is there anything else you'd like to know?
- » What do you think are my strongest assets and possible weaknesses?
- » Do you have any concerns that I need to clear up in order to be a considered candidate?

## Questions About the Recruiter

Asking recruiters about their views and experience in the job or working with the airline will demonstrate your genuine interest and motives.

- » How did you find the transition in relocating to ...?
- » Why did you choose to work at ... airlines?
- » What is it about this airline that keeps you working here?
- » It sounds as if you really enjoy working here, what have you enjoyed most about working for ... airlines?

## General Questions

- » How would you describe the company culture?
- » I feel my background and experience are a good fit for this position, and I am very interested. What is the next step?
- » Yes, when do I start?

## No Questions

- » I did have plenty of questions, but we've covered them all during our discussions. I was particularly interested in ... but we've dealt with that thoroughly.
- » I had many questions, but you've answered them all you have been so helpful. I'm even more excited about this opportunity than when I applied.

## Questions to Avoid

You should avoid asking questions such as those following as they will make you appear selfishly motivated.

- » How many day's holiday allowances will I receive?
- » What is the salary?
- » When will I receive a pay increase?
- » How many free flights will my family receive?
- » Can I request flights to ...?

# THE
# CONCLUSION
## WHAT NEXT?

# What happens NEXT?

Following the final interview, airlines aim to follow up with candidates within two to eight weeks. This is the time that is most difficult, and it is unlikely that you will sleep soundly as you wait of the outome of the interview.

If you are successful, you can expect to receive a job offer from the recruitment department by email, telephone and/or letter within the noted time frame. ,

For those candidates who have been successful, you will be advised of the various pre joining clearance requirements. These may include:

Preemployment medical test
Reference checks
Joining forms

Once the required steps of the process have been completed, the airline will make the necessary arrangements to deliver the employment contract and relevant documentation. You will also be given final clearance to resign from your current employer.

# Coping with
## SETBACKS

It may seem counter intuitive to provide coping strategies for rejection in an interview guidance book, however, in an industry such as this, where supply exceeds demand, rejection is an unfortunate outcome that some candidates will ultimately face.

So, rather than be crushed by this outcome, I have put together the following tips for coping with, learning from and moving forward following a setback.

## Prepare

The popular saying 'Prepare for the worst, but hope for the best' certainly applies in interview scenarios. If you attend the interview with an open mind, your attitude will be more relaxed, you will be better prepared and your coping abilities will be greatly enhanced.

## Assess

Faced with rejection, it can be easy to misplace blame on yourself, others or on the general circumstances. But, if you are to learn and grow from your experience, you must be objective and logical in your assessment, rather than making rash and unsubstantiated assumptions.

Firstly, you need to reflect on your own performance to establish any possible areas for improvement. You can then make adjustments as necessary and shift your focus to the next opportunity.

Firstly, you need to reflect on your own performance to establish any possible areas for improvement. In this assessment, you could ask:

Did I dress appropriately?
How did I sound?
Did I arrive on time?
Did I remember to smile?
Did I appear confident and relaxed?
Could my answers have been improved?
Did I maintain appropriate eye contact?
Did I establish rapport with the recruiter?

If this assessment identifies any weaknesses, you can make adjustments as necessary and shift your focus to the next opportunity.

# Accept

Sometimes factors exist that are beyond your control and the unfortunate outcome may not have been directly influenced by your performance at all. In this instance, all you can do is accept the outcome and shift your focus to the next opportunity.

# Be positive

Whatever the reason for rejection, it is important to treat each setback as a learning experience. So, don't become obsessive or overly critical, keep an open mind and be open to change if necessary. By handling the setback in this way, you will move forward and succeed much more quickly.

# I would love
## TO HEAR FROM YOU

If you have enjoyed reading this guide and have found it useful, I would love to hear from you, so please consider leaving your feedback.

www.CabinCrew.Guide

Where dreams are made

Facebook

# Coming
## SOON . . .

Cabin Crew Interview ANSWERS
Made Easy

www.CabinCrew.Guide

Where dreams are made

Printed by BoD™in Norderstedt, Germany